Stress
SOULutions

Mind Body Techniques

Finding Your Peace and Calm

NIOMI REARDON

First published by Ultimate World Publishing 2019
Copyright © 2019 Niomi Reardon

Niomi Reardon has asserted her right under the Copyright, Designs and Patents Act 1988 to be identified as the author of this work. The information in this book is based on the author's experiences and opinions. The publisher specifically disclaims responsibility for any adverse consequences, which may result from use of the information contained herein. The information used has been interpreted by the author and is the authors opinion. Any breaches will be rectified in further editions of the book. The author apologises for any misinterpretation of work cited.

All rights reserved. No part of this publication may be reproduced, stored in or introduced into a retrieval system, or transmitted in any form, or by any means (electronic, mechanical, photocopying, recording or otherwise) without the prior written permission of the author. Any person who does any unauthorised act in relation to this publication may be liable to criminal prosecution and civil claims for damages. Enquiries should be made through the publisher.

Cover design: Ultimate World Publishing
Layout and typesetting: Ultimate World Publishing
Editor: Marinda Wilkinson
Photographer: Craig Arnold

Ultimate World Publishing
Diamond Creek,
Victoria Australia 3089
www.writeabook.com.au

Testimonials

In her book Stress Soulutions, Niomi reminds us how important it is to practice self-care. Anyone who wants to take control of their health mentally, physically and spiritually should read this book. It will change the way you care for yourself and your loved ones, by prioritising health. Niomi teaches us how to implement NLP, intuition, meditation and mindfulness in our daily life. I highly recommend this book for nurses and anyone working in the healthcare field to read and apply the suggestions to take control of your life and live happy, healthy and prosperous.
Lillian Gonzalez, Family Nurse Practitioner & Author of Help Yourself: A Nurse's Guide to Implementing Self-Care

The power of the mind and body when in harmony is truly magnificent. At the time of writing, one in three women will experience anxiety and one in six will suffer from depression.

Stress and burnout are familiar feelings for a large majority of people, especially women. Niomi has developed a comprehensive program with effective stress management techniques for having a greater self-awareness and understanding. By acknowledging the power of the mind/body connection, she guides readers through strategies to promote peace and happiness. A truly beautiful practitioner, I highly recommend reading this book and sharing it with a friend.

Tracy Tully, Founder of Motivation and Resilience for Women

In this book, Niomi Reardon challenges the reader to view their relationship in understanding personal stress through a different lens. She articulates the physiological and psychological benefits of stress within our lives and the importance of self-awareness in managing ourselves through stressful experiences. With reference to research in this important area Niomi offers strategies and suggestions for enhancing wellness through life's challenges. I commend Niomi for sharing her knowledge and trust readers will find ways of integrating her advice to the betterment of their own lives. Congratulations Niomi on writing this book.

Dr Jo Lukins, Author of The Elite: Think like an Athlete, Succeed like a Champion

Stress Soulutions is a useful, fun and interesting view of stress management. This book integrates the new concepts of epigenetics and nervous system health with more traditional types of meditation and energy healing. Everyone should have this information at their fingertips, not only as a personal reference, but to assist in the decrease of stress levels within our society. I highly recommend reading this book and sharing it with anyone who suffers from stress and anxiety.

Donna King, Registered Nurse

I found Stress Soulutions to be a beautifully written book full of great information, gentle reminders, guidance and practical solutions. I loved the actions for the reader. So proactive and allows the information read to be consolidated and easily incorporated into daily life. This book is a great tool for anybody wanting to live their best life.

Fiona McWhirter, Registered Nurse, Mother of 5, Wife & Trauma Survivor

Dedication

To everyone who chooses to contribute to world peace one step at a time via inner calm and human compassion.

Also dedicated to my pioneering loving parents Kym and Lin who taught me the potential of magic and making your own path when the road most travelled is not appealing.

To my sister Daina and my friends that are like family and make up my tribe of people to have fun with.

And to my husband Sean and children Elysha, Sunira and Kiara. You inspire me every day to lead an extraordinary life with a goal to love mother earth and show kindness to every inhabitant.

Contents

Testimonials iii

Dedication vi

Introduction x

Chapter 1 - Healthy Relaxed Living: Explores the undisputable connection between stress and illness and how you can achieve ultimate health throughout your life 1

Chapter 2 - Thank Your Pain: Learn the language that our bodies speak so you can understand and interpret the messages and act early to stay well 15

Chapter 3 - Feel Good Formula: Understanding the science behind cancer prevention. This could save your life 26

Chapter 4 - Busting the Myths: Your genes do not determine your health. So, now you know… what next? Learn to utilise neuroscience and accelerate your strengths 40

Chapter 5 - The Art of Following Your Intuition: The most powerful person in your life is you. Learn simple but powerful techniques to harness this 50

Chapter 6 - Utilising Energy Medicine: Combining old and new knowledge, to determine what is best for you 63

Chapter 7 - You Can Change Your Life With NLP: Neurolinguistic programming can be simple, fun and life-changing 77

Chapter 8 - Your Sensational Nervous System: When you learn how this works, you will understand why you react the way you do. Both the good and the bad 84

Chapter 9 - Abundant Energy: Is your energy being zapped by stress and you are not even aware of it? Learn the signs and the treatments 102

Chapter 10 - Meditation and Mindfulness for the Soul: Learn the basics of meditation and mindfulness for everyday use. No blank mind required 119

Chapter 11 - **What Happens in Vagus:** An introduction to the underestimated vagus nerve and how to harness its power ………………………………………………………….... 132

Chapter 12 - **The Magic of Intention:** How to improve your day by simply asking for a good day in the right way …..… 143

References and Recommended Reading List ………….... 157

About the Author …………………………………………. 162

Offer 1 …………………………………………………..... 165

Offer 2 …………………………………………………..... 168

Offer 3 …………………………………………………..... 171

Testimonials ……………………………………………… 172

Introduction

This book is designed to be opened at any chapter. It has come about because of my innate desire to reduce suffering in the world and promote peace and happiness in you.

If every one of us can work on our own sense of inner calm, we can cause a ripple of peace throughout the universe. A life full of unicorns, sunsets and rainbows may not be realistic, but a better understanding of human emotions and compassion for all beings is achievable.

If you can become calmer and more informed after reading this book, then my mission is accomplished. In the process you may find that you end up with all your ducks in a row. May you dwell in peace and joy and witness many sunsets.

Stress SOULutions

Chapter 1
Healthy Relaxed Living

'It is not stress that kills us, it is our reaction to it.'
Hans Selye

There is overwhelming evidence that the world is becoming a better place to live. It's an exciting time to be a human being. Women have the best opportunities ever in history. Poverty is decreasing. Our health care and life expectancy is the best it has ever been. Child mortality is declining. Literacy is on the rise. The human species is making incredible progress.

The devastating irony is that although we have never had it so good, we have never been so depressed and lacking a sense of peace on earth. The biggest health challenge facing the world right now is from the effects of stress on individuals and communities. Even the best healthcare facilities in the world are unable to address this new crisis. The volume of depressed and anxious people has become so great that we need to listen as a collective human species and respond accordingly. Depression and anxiety do not discriminate. It is time to integrate caring techniques into everyday life so that they are as common and natural as brushing your teeth and having a shower.

We have now come to realise that aside from the flu, Ebola and other acute infectious epidemics, the greatest danger to our mortality, our overall health and our economy, is stress and stress-related diseases.

Stress reduces our metabolic reserve and increases the chance of what we call 'metabolic syndrome' which includes obesity, high cholesterol, high blood pressure, diabetes and other chronic stress-related diseases. If we want to address this challenge, we all need to play our part.

By learning to love and manage your stress, you can decrease your risks of cancer, improve your quality of sleep, boost your immune system, build your resilience and increase your happiness. And by modelling lower stress to those around us, teaching it to others and bringing techniques into schools, workplaces and homes, we can help ourselves and others to live a longer, higher quality of life and essentially spread a ripple of universal peace to everybody in the world. These are lofty, but realistic, goals for all!

I was inspired to write this book because of the condition of many people's mental health, particularly those caring for others. In a

Stress SOULutions

recent study of nurses in NSW, over 40% were found to suffer from at least one form of chronic disease, including anxiety and depression (Perry, Gallagher & Duffield 2015). While I initially set out to write this book for nurses, as it came together, I realised the information is relevant to people from all professions and walks of life who could benefit from learning stress-relieving skills and increased compassion.

Depression is the most extreme form of stress and the World Health Organisation (WHO) reports that it is the leading cause of disability and a major contributor to ill health worldwide. They also predict that the number of people who experience depression will continue to increase over the next few years.

The problem is partly because we do not know enough about the effects of stress on our mind and body. How do you assess your own stress levels? How do you gauge if they are healthy? Are you waiting until it is too late before you respond because you are failing to recognise the signs?

The connection between stress and illness is indisputable. Caring is a stressful and draining job, and almost everybody cares for someone, somehow. If you have a child, a friend, a spouse, a pet or a co-worker, you very likely care for others. Chances are that you care for that pet or child better than you care for yourself. Until recently, we've never been taught how to care for others without draining our own reserves.

HOW STRESS HELPS US

There is a true positive purpose for stress. Without a stress response and the ability to jump out of harm's way, humans would be worse off. Stress also has the ability to improve performance in all of us at certain times. An example of this is when the elite athlete finds that extra something to get them over the finish line or when a parent reacts with lightning speed to stop their child burning themselves on a fire.

In an emergency your adrenal gland squirts some adrenaline out and you react, possibly faster than you have in months or maybe years. You can thank your body for this, as it's an automatic reaction, with little or no thought required.

Being grateful for a stress response is lesson number one. Learning how to be aware of the negative stress that needs attention requires more focus, and that is the purpose of this book. I will share techniques that will allow you to tame your negative stress, so you can use and decrease it for your advantage, for optimal, authentic and engaged living.

UNDERSTANDING STRESS

As a starting point, it is helpful to understand what stress is and how it affects your body and mind. There are essentially three types of stress: physical, chemical, and emotional.

Stress SOULutions

Physical stress is obvious, it's the damage your body sustains when you cut your arm or you break your leg.

Chemical stress relates to how factors such as the food you eat and the thoughts you have change the chemical reactions in your brain.

Emotional stress is how you feel when you're in traffic jams, while parenting, after losing a loved one, that sort of thing.

All humans can tolerate short-term stress quite wellhowever, when the stress is experienced over longer periods, it becomes an issue.

Your level of understanding and beliefs about stress can also potentially save your life. Research cited by psychologist Kelly McGonigal in her TED talk in 2013, shows that by simply understanding and cognitively realising that stress in its correct form, is healthy, can prevent stress- related diseases.

In the study, people who experienced a lot of stress and who felt it was harmful to their health, increased their risk of a premature death by 43% (Keller et al. 2012). However, those who experienced a lot of stress but did not view it as harmful were found to be the least likely to die early.

Another controlled experiment measured the association of physical stress responses such as an unhealthy elevated heart rate and blood vessel constriction with cardiovascular disease. Once again, the participants that learned to see the response as healthy were less anxious, more confident and remarkably, their blood vessels stayed relaxed. In fact, their responses were closer to joy and courage than stress (Jamieson, Nock & Mendes 2012).

So, start believing stress is ok and you will be fine. No need to read any further. You are welcome. So simple, so effective!

If only it really was that simple.

UNCOVERING TECHNIQUES THAT CAN HELP

I was inspired to write this book after 30 years of working as a registered nurse. My experiences caring for the sick and injured, helping students become registered nurses and talking to and coaching people who care for others made me realise that most of us were never taught how to manage stress effectively.

As a young nurse I was constantly sick, and always had something wrong with my basic health. I developed stomach inflammation that required medication and I experienced hypertension, which required medication. I became passionate about learning ways to combat this stress and discovered that there are so many simple and enjoyable techniques that hardly anybody knows about. Not all of it is easy; some tasks require commitment, perseverance and some serious soul-searching. I've made it my mission to educate and help

others so that they may not suffer some of the similar stress results that I have witnessed and experienced.

It is indisputable that stress and the mind-body connection can prevent or cause disease. Stress causes brainwaves to function in a way that is like driving your car in first gear up and down hills constantly until it eventually breaks down. If you have only ever driven an automatic, it is like driving with the brake and the accelerator on at the same time. While this can create a lot of work for mechanics (or doctors) which may be a positive for them, it is certainly not ideal for us!

My mission is to teach everybody and anybody, fun and effective ways to maintain stress at a healthy level. In this book I'll share insights and techniques that will help you to learn:

- How the mind-body connection relates to your experience of personal pain.
- Why meditation and mindfulness is important (even for the sceptic).
- Some simple but effective cancer prevention techniques you can introduce to your daily life.
- What exceptional humans can teach us about understanding and preventing stress and disease.

It is amazing how a basic understanding of epigenetics, and its ability to change our health by the way we process feelings and thoughts can completely alter your way of functioning. I am also excited to enlighten people about utilising energy medicine, maximising trauma resilience and maintaining or commencing self-care – hallelujah for neuroscience and its reproducible scientific experiments!

It is also poignant to touch on protecting yourself, both emotionally and physically. I have found that most, or many, nurses and people in the caring profession are empaths. When you are an empath, you very likely absorb the stresses of other people, and this can cause empathy or compassion fatigue. Preventing burnout is crucial to every one of us, and when you truly love and care for yourself it is very difficult to harm yourself. But how do you even know if you are in a healthy stress range? Learning the signs and responding in helpful ways is the biggest revolution in preventative health care.

LEARNING TO LISTEN TO OUR BODY

One of the biggest awakenings for me was understanding how the nervous system works, and how to work with it. Our bodies can tell us so much, if we can only learn to tune in and listen.

If you suffer regularly from any of the following symptoms, there is a high chance you are carrying too much stress in your life:

- frequent colds and infections
- insomnia
- low energy

- anxiety
- poor concentration
- mood swings
- recurrent nightmares or flashbacks
- headaches
- gastric disturbances such as diarrhea or constipation
- nausea
- aches, pains and tense muscles
- autoimmune disorders
- rapid heartbeat
- other mystery symptoms.

All of us are at risk of developing one or more of the stress-related non-communicable diseases that are so prevalent today. Educating ourselves, both personally and as a society, is our greatest weapon in prevention. Also, teaching our children about stress and how to better manage it through self-care techniques is an important way that we can make a huge and positive change in the world.

One of the biggest breakthroughs for me personally was to understand and to utilise body scanning. I suffered from chronic pain for many years, and yes it had a physical reason (and there are X-rays to prove it). After surgeons told me I needed an operation, I became concerned, as pain that persists long after it is helpful is very complex and exhausting. I realised that if I wasn't careful, I could potentially become addicted to medication. I was very wary of this and sought any way to decrease the use of pain-relieving medication. During this time, I learnt a great deal about the brain and its response to pain, to the point where I rarely need analgesia anymore.

The body scanning technique is what saved me. I realised that my pain was intensified in moments of stress, and if I could just stop, scan, and think about this pain and how I would benefit if it would stop, I could turn down my pain receptors. With practice, this technique can be done within about 30 seconds and it is quite possible for most people to do. However, I do not suggest that anyone should stop taking medication if they need it.

Learning about storing stress within the body and how to discard it is also very valuable. As the saying goes, 'the issues are in your tissues'. This type of stress is often referred to as trauma, which I will examine further later in the book. We all have some form of trauma storage, which can turn into disease if it is not dealt with in a loving, appropriate way.

I have seen this firsthand while caring for people in hospital who are experiencing extreme pain, and often chronic pain. If the opportunity is there to just sit and listen, to understand why they have their pain and allow them to verbalise it, often the pain will decrease. This will not always remove the need for painkillers, but it can decrease the need for them where appropriate. If you feel heard and understand that you have some control over your level of

chronic pain, this alone has the power to turn down your pain receptors.

All of us could benefit from cultivating an awareness called 'interoception', which is simply being able to sense, or tune in to what your physiology is doing. When you have a perception of your internal physiology, you will be more aware of your stress chemistry, acknowledging the strain, and acknowledging the ease. When we know which to pay attention to, then we can shut the gate before the horses bolt, rather than afterwards.

A lack of interoception in First World countries seems to be contributing to so much of our stress. A basic explanation of this is when you feel grumpy or angry and realise it is because you haven't eaten recently. In fact, the word 'hangry' was created because of this! If you are one of those people who are prone to feeling hangry, you have likely adapted to decrease its impact on your life. However, you may notice it in others who haven't figured it out yet.

Too often these days, we push things down and pretend they didn't happen. When we get a headache, we take a couple of paracetamols and keep going. In order to push on and achieve, we've become completely disconnected from our own body.

Does this sound like you? Do you ignore messages from your body until something becomes big enough that it needs more intense treatment? Do you say you value health over wealth and yet continue to sacrifice your health for wealth? Underlying stress will persist when you are not living to your true values.

That's why techniques like body scanning, yoga, meditation, mindfulness exercises and tai chi can bring you back into contact with who you really are. There are reasons why having some allocated worry time, learning how to breathe in particular ways and exercising regularly can reduce your stress levels and contribute to your ultimate health.

It's now time to learn new behaviours. Isn't it amazing how we can think about something horrible, or something wonderful that happened a while ago, and get those feelings straight back? We can turn on our stress by thought alone. We can also turn off our stress by thought alone. I think most of us can improve on our stress management. I have learnt to completely change my relationship to stress and I am very lucky, that I haven't had a bad cold or a flu in 10 years. I am medication free and I accredit this partly to many of the stress techniques that I have trained in.

If you think you don't have time to learn about stress techniques, then you may be forced to make time to be ill. If we as a society continue on the same path that we're on now, and the World Health Organisation predictions are correct, then in 2020 we'll have even more stress-related problems than we already have currently. However, it's not all doom and gloom. We as a collective

human species have a desire to evolve and that's what we're doing. Our brains are continually developing, and so can we.

Unfortunately, many people go through life living by the hormones of stress, and when you don't know any different, you think it's normal. If you truly know and love yourself, it is very difficult to treat yourself badly. If we can decrease our baseline of stress then we will be able to pass this on to our children, our family, colleagues and all we meet. We will also feel happier, healthier and have less disease.

So, what can you do? You can read the other chapters and learn the techniques that have saved my health and the health of my clients. Be open to the possibilities of self-development and human evolution. Slowly become aware of whether your nervous system is overly sensitised. We all have a certain capacity that changes according to our life and the stage that we're in, and this resilience can be improved and increased – and this is wonderful.

3 helpful actions to take after reading this chapter:

1. Befriend your stress with an attitude of gratitude. Stress is a helpful messenger. Aim to improve your use of stress rather than remove it.

2. Examine your attitudes to stress and think about how you detect and respond to signs that your body and mind are sending you. Note any unique signs you may get. For example, I find my feet ache as soon as they touch the floor in the morning when my stress levels are rising, even when I don't think I am stressed. If I don't act then and implement some care strategies, I get the next sign and so on. What subtle messages do you get?

3. Have an open mind about all the latest incredible science-based techniques to improve health.

Chapter 2

Thank Your Pain

'The pain it will leave once it has finished teaching you.' Pavana

Taking control of your stress can help you manage and understand your pain and discomfort. Your mind and body are not separate. Learning to recognise and effectively treat pain and the underlying symptoms your body is trying to tell you can benefit you in so many ways, helping you to maintain your enjoyment of life, not just exist. It can also help to prevent serious or chronic disease, teach you a better work-life balance and ultimately, decrease suicide risk, depression and anxiety.

Did you know that pain is the most common reason that people seek medical help? Yet according to Painaustralia, it remains the most neglected and misunderstood area of health care. Over three million Australian adults live with chronic pain (Pezzullo 2019), and chronic pain also affects adolescents and children. Pain and stress are related. If you have an illness there may also be some emotional issues in your mind you need to work through and address. My pain was connected to anxiety and sleep deprivation.

Almost everyone will say at the start, 'oh no that's not me' and, 'my pain is proven by the X-rays'. While this may be correct, it is still important to realise that your pain is trying to tell you something and if you work out the message it will likely decrease. Your subconscious may be telling you to slow down, eat better, exercise more or even face the traumas of your past and deal with them once and for all. It will try in many ways to get the message across, until eventually it shows up in an illness.

It's currently impossible to determine why two seemingly similar people can have such different health challenges. My dear friend and oncology nurse says that it's mostly nice people that get cancer. This is in itself a complex issue. Life is not fair. It is agonising, cruel, messy, sad, devastating and confusing whilst also being exquisitely beautiful, loving, kind, tender, joyful and a huge gift we have all received. The challenge lies in examining every possibility and learning to listen to the language of life on earth and within the self. A language without words or ego.

Neuroscientist Joseph LeDoux and his colleagues have shown that the only way we can consciously access the emotional brain is through self-awareness. This happens by activating the medial prefrontal cortex which is the part of the brain that notices what is

going on inside us. This helps us to identify what we're feeling, and eventually why we're feeling it – and it might not be what you think it is.

Neuroscience research tells us that the only way we can change the way we feel is by becoming aware of our inner experience and learning to befriend what is going on inside ourselves. Mindfulness teaches this skill.

THE RELATIONSHIP BETWEEN PAIN AND STRESS

So, the facts are, that stress and pain feed each other. As pain and stress expert Jennifer Schneider MD, PhD, author of *Living with Chronic Pain* explains, 'each makes the other worse'. This means, that if you can decrease one, you will likely also decrease the other.

Because pain is regulated by the nervous system, the brain is a key player in how we perceive pain. The brain is always trying to inhibit pain signals, but if you're stressed, the brain's ability to filter these pain signals is affected in a really negative way and pain can be increased. The exception is in acute trauma such as accidental amputation in a battle or accident where the adrenaline kicks in and nothing is felt for a short time.

I'd like to focus on the term **interoception**, which is broadly defined as 'the sense of the internal state of the body or sensitivity to stimuli originating inside of the body'. It encompasses the brain's process of integrating signals relayed from the body into specific subregions allowing for a representation of the physiological state of the body. This is important for maintaining an equilibrium in the body and potentially aiding in self-awareness. In other words, it's the art of looking inside and learning to identify what you see inside yourself with accuracy.

How often do we go about our days feeling things within our body and trying to determine their cause, yet never really finding an answer? We might go so far as to see a doctor or a physiotherapist in an attempt to explain what's going on. We might complain of pain in our shoulders or some sort of tightness in our knees, or maybe a stomach-ache that's unexplained. There's no doubt that sometimes these problems are simply because you've eaten the wrong thing, or maybe you've walked too far, or jumped in a silly way, but it's also important to consider our state of mind and our emotions and how these translate into physical symptoms.

Working in a hospital you deal with people in pain on a daily basis. During one unusually quiet night shift an elderly patient requested some pain relief. She was obviously in pain; her face was screwed up and she was tensing up. I happened to be lucky enough to have time to sit and talk to her. I opened her chart and saw that she was due painkillers and asked her to explain where the pain was, and why she thought the pain was there. She looked at me and said, 'Well, it's the reason I'm here, I'm not well'. I gently replied 'Yes,

but can you tell me exactly where your pain is, and why you have it?'. After some conversation and confused looks from her she took a deep breath and said, 'I really just miss my mother'. We had a long discussion and she told me about the sadness she felt on the loss of her mother.

At that point, I realised that we'd been chatting for over 10 minutes. I said to her, 'Would you like your painkillers now?' and she said, 'Actually, I think I can wait a little bit longer now, thank you'. I asked if she was sure (as nurses know we do have the gate control theory of pain, which I'll explain in a minute) and she replied, 'Yes, I'm sure. I know that if I need something, I can ring the bell and you'll come to me'.

A few days later when I was working in a different area, I didn't recognise her as she called out to me, 'Hey, I remember you, you were that angel that helped me with my pain'. This is just one of the highlights of being able to talk to people and help with healing, but it's also an example of the body and mind connection. As a sidenote I also got hit in the head accidentally by a confused patient that same week – just to balance the reality of the job!

Now back to the gate control theory. In the medical system, we are generous with pain relief because it has been shown in research that if people are left in pain, they may heal slower because they tend to keep still, which can lead to decreased movement long-term. It's also thought that providing regular pain relief can reduce the need for stronger painkillers. For example, if a fenced yard on a farm is full of wild horses and the gate is opened just slightly, the horses will flee. However, if you notice the gate is slightly open and latch it up quickly, then none will escape. Your pain response can be similar. If the pain begins to get too strong, it can feel like the wild horses are bolting and you're going to struggle to shut that gate – which means, you'll need higher and higher doses of painkillers.

With the above examples, I am not advocating for or against the use of analgesia and painkillers as I believe they have their place and should be used relevant to the symptoms. What I'm getting at is, next time you notice a bit of a headache or sore back and *you have the ability to pay attention to this pain*, rest, make space for the tension, try some interoception and you may find it eases.

The key point to all of this is, that if you focus on prevention and take note of your symptoms and what they are telling you, then you'll spend less time healing. Prevention is always better than the cure.

Here's a little saying I heard once (author unknown), which I feel rings true:

Either way we spend the time; we either take care of and maintain our bodies and mind, or we work to repair, investigate and heal our bodies and mind. Either way, we spend the time.

IMAGINE YOUR PAIN AWAY

Another thing to consider is that pain and symptoms can become a habit. We all have programs that we run in our mind. It doesn't mean that you consciously chose the pain or you like it, but it may become a habit through no logical choice of your own. Focusing on how life feels without this pain and visualising yourself without it is one way to combat this.

Most people working in the medical profession would have come across the phenomenon of phantom pain. For example, when a person has had their leg amputated and feels pain not at the site where their limb was amputated, but rather in their toe. They logically know their toe is not there, but the pain feels real. It's a fascinating phenomenon to examine, and it provides a good example of the mind-body connection.

Right now, you may be thinking that focusing on pain doesn't seem like a positive move. Surely that's just going to make it worse if you focus on it all the time? And to a degree that can be correct; but generally, ignoring pain makes it persist. Modern medicine is amazing, there is no doubt about that. We have wonderful painkillers that are effective, cheap and work fast. So, why wouldn't you just take painkillers every time you're in pain and just move on? Modern life demands that we work hard and we keep going.

While that's okay occasionally, if you're needing to do this often, not only will the effectiveness of the painkillers decrease, there's also a high risk of addiction and the potential side effects of damaged liver or kidneys.

On top of this, what we resist will persist. Pain is the body talking to you and if you can't figure out what is causing the pain it may get worse. If you are becoming psychologically disconnected from your body by living on autopilot, pain can be a way that your soul pulls you back and reminds you that you are a physical body having an earthly experience. It is a lot harder to function in a state of emotional numbness when your body is screaming in pain. Have you ever been acutely sick with an awful gastro bug for 24 hours? Then the next day when it's all over the world suddenly seems like a wonderful and beautiful place? It is possible to maintain that feeling of joy and gratitude in being healthy each day.

'Be grateful for what you have; you'll end up having more.' Oprah Winfrey

If you don't believe pain is emotional at all and that it is just something physical that is not mind-body connected, think again. A study of brain X-rays showed that social discomfort and physical pain produce similar responses in the brain. I can attest to this, especially during my past experiences of being uncomfortable in crowds.

In my early working years, I would always put my patients before myself. Even if I was hungry, in pain or hadn't been to the toilet all shift, I always focused on my patients first. This attitude was a key contributor to most of my health problems. It's the old cliché of learning to put the oxygen mask on yourself before you put it on the child next to you in an aeroplane emergency. If we don't care for ourselves, we will not be as effective when caring for others. It is logical that a hungry, tired, dehydrated worker is not as astute. Such a simple lesson, but it took me many years to figure out. Thank goodness the world now has more awareness of this.

Self-esteem and confidence also play a part in removing personal stress in this scenario. Applying self-compassion for past poor self-care and moving on is the message here.

SMALL ADJUSTMENTS, BIG BENEFITS

What can we learn from all these examples? The skill of interoception and learning to do regular body scans has huge potential for disease prevention and pain relief. Right now, as you read these words, what could you adjust to improve some tension in your body? As I'm currently typing I mindfully drop my shoulders away from my ears.

If you take the time to learn these helpful techniques and eventually are doing them frequently, this will flow on to create further adjustments to your thought processes and physical stance – and when it comes to prevention, this is huge. Search online for body scanning techniques (there are hundreds), find one that you like and listen until it becomes natural. It's a good idea to do this at night as you fall asleep when you are first starting. YouTube has some wonderful free options to listen to. With practice, it becomes a fast, effective tool in reducing pain and anxiety. Learning to pay attention to your body's messages is one of the most valuable forms of prevention in health care.

Hypnosis and self-hypnosis are invaluable when done with an open mind. Although it is not technically embraced in a hospital setting, I have had surprising success whenever I have asked people if they would like my 'help' in tolerating a procedure. I omit the word hypnosis but remain ethical because all hypnosis is self-hypnosis. There are hundreds of free hypnosis tracks online, for every condition you can think of. One of my favourites apps is Insight Timer. It is often labelled as meditation but can be adapted as hypnosis. You'll need internet access to listen, or you can purchase a single track for less than $20 and have it with you anywhere, anytime on your phone or device. I am so incredibly grateful for this service – it's like having your own therapist everywhere you go.

Journaling can also help if you have pain that is reoccurring, as you can record your thoughts and feelings and see if there is a pattern or hidden explanation. For example, what were you thinking right before your pain started? Pain is often related to stress or events, and if you can figure out what's going on and address this, you may

be able to turn your pain off or down. The connection between the mind and writing things on paper can be a game changer. Journaling can be helpful for bringing good things into your life as well as removing things from your existence.

First think about the pain, and then write about the origins of it. You may not have any ideas to start with, but sometimes unexplained pain can be relieved by going back and remembering a past trauma or injury. If it is long-term pain and no longer useful to your survival, what do you need to acknowledge for it to ease?

3 helpful actions to take after reading this chapter:

1. Become aware of your interoception and start a journal to create gratitude and remove pain.

2. Learn and practise the basics of body scanning. The guided body scan meditations by Jon Kabat-Zinn on YouTube are a good place to start.

3. Try self-hypnosis techniques or meditation to gain insight into your pain or illness.

Chapter 3
Feel Good Formula

'May your choices reflect your hopes not your fears.' Nelson Mandela

Miracles are finally being scientifically documented and studied so that we can aim to replicate them. When I first heard about the Spontaneous Remission Project, I was aghast that this was so barely known about. It is a scientific study of incredible cancer (and potentially terminal illness) recoveries. The justification for not promoting this incredible life-changing or even life-saving information came down to medical experts claiming they 'don't want to give people false hope'.

Thank goodness for those who persevered to get this information to the common people. Initially it seemed that society accepted fear as a motivation but not potential hope as a motivator. This has all changed, thanks to a few dedicated intelligent, compassionate, science-based people.

Stress SOULutions

In 1993, the Institute of Noetic Sciences published *Spontaneous Remission: An Annotated Bibliography*. In this work, the authors defined spontaneous remission as 'the disappearance, complete or incomplete, of a disease or cancer without medical treatment or treatment that is considered inadequate to produce the resulting disappearance of disease symptoms or tumours'.

The remission project catalogued the medical literature, and the resulting book was the largest database of medically reported cases of spontaneous remission in the world. It includes more than 3,500 references from 800 journals in 20 languages, however, the numbers are now much higher and the database is increasing continually. All of these people have recovered, with medical proof via X-rays, blood results and MRIs which have been verified by experts.

Why should we even care about these studies when we have such wonderful medical treatment for people with cancer? Did you know that cancer is the second leading cause of death globally? The World Health Organisation also believes that one-third of deaths from cancer are due to one (or more) of the five leading behaviour and dietary risks: high body mass index (BMI), low fruit and vegetable intake, not enough exercise, too much alcohol and smoking.

As yet, the dimension of stress has not been included in these statistics, but there are many people working on research as you read. Early findings do show that stress is a likely contributor and

your condition may become worse if you don't have your stress under control and you have any form of cancer in your body.

For the continued progression of the human race as we evolve, we need to gain a better understanding of cancer – not just what it does to our bodies, but importantly, how and why we get it. It is obvious what a bonus it would be to have less cancer in the world, as the quality and quantity of life will increase. Understanding the survival techniques is the same as applying prevention techniques – because they are the same techniques.

Studying cancer prevention is one way to give people hope, but there has been many a time when I've been supporting someone who has a new diagnosis of cancer, and the amount of information they are given is overwhelming. I've always wanted to have something that gives them more hope rather than just explaining the treatment. If it was possible to provide a small overview of the radical remission project on diagnosis, I think that would be very helpful.

NINE HABITS THAT COULD SAVE YOUR LIFE

When I came across Kelly Turner's book, *Radical Remission: Surviving Cancer Against All Odds*, I was ecstatic. For her dissertation research, she interviewed people who had experienced radical remission to gain an understanding of how they healed.

Stress SOULutions

While some people had used up to 30 different techniques or methods to heal, she identified nine key things that every single one of them had done.

She was not the first to study this information and if you are interested to learn more, the book *Spontaneous Healing* by Andrew Weil is an interesting read. They both cite some similar documented cases that are fascinating.

Turner defines radical remission if any of the following have occurred:

- A cancer goes away without the patient using any conventional medicine
- A cancer patient tries conventional medicine, but the cancer does not go into remission, so they switch to alternative methods of healing, which do lead to remission
- A cancer patient uses conventional medicine and alternative healing methods at the same time in order to outlive a statistically dire prognosis such as any cancer with a less than 25% or five-year survival prediction

Most of the people cited in the book had been told that medically, there was nothing more that could be done. They then chose to make the nine (or more) changes in their lives and their cancer went into remission. Obviously, it's not quite that easy (how wonderful if it was!), but unexpected remissions are real. Thousands of people have experienced them, and we can use this information to replicate their actions and behaviour for prevention.

I'm disappointed that as a society, we spend so much money, research and time on studying cures and not so much time on prevention. This study is a wonderful example of how we can focus our research on healing and use it to our advantage for prevention.

For curiosity's sake, I will explain the nine areas that Kelly Turner identified as the key factors for radical remission. During her study, she analysed all her cases carefully and repeatedly, using qualitative research methods. She identified more than 75 different factors that may hypothetically have played a role in the radical remission. However, when she looked at the frequency of each factor, she saw that these nine factors kept coming up again and again. They are (in no particular order):

1. Radically changing your diet

2. Taking control of your health

3. Following your intuition

4. Using herbs and supplements

5. Releasing suppressed emotions

6. Increasing positive emotions

7. Embracing social support

Stress SOULutions

8. Deepening your spiritual connection

9. Having strong reasons for living

Surprisingly, most of these are emotional. There was no clear standout from all of these, they were all just mentioned very frequently.

In one remission case, a patient talks about being forced to face his own fear of death. He was diagnosed with stage four lymphoplasmacytic lymphoma, which is a very rare and hard to treat form of lymphoma. He attempted some chemotherapy, but it made his cancer grow, so he decided to stop chemotherapy and instead pursue alternative medicine.

He was told that he only had one to two years to live, so he then embarked on a healing journey, which included energy treatments from various healers, herbal supplements and a commitment to releasing all trauma from his past and all fear from his present. He describes how he couldn't sleep for about four days and then eventually when he could accept reality and went through this process of facing his fear and accepting that he was going to die, his healing began. Nathan's doctors gave him one to two years to live in 2005. When he was interviewed in 2011, he was enjoying travelling and soaking up the world.

Obviously, facing a fear of death can range from being mildly to tremendously difficult, depending on what you believe. Turner does mention that in almost all the radical remission survivors she spoke with, facing their fear directly at least for a short while gave them some degree of relief because they were no longer ignoring the elephant in the room.

THE NINE FACTORS IN ACTION

A further example of how much power fear has over the physical body, is shown in a study where researchers were trying a new type of chemotherapy. They separated cancer patients into two randomised groups. The first group received the new chemotherapy, while the second control group thought they were getting the new chemotherapy but were only receiving saline infusions. Now listen to this. Amazingly, 30% (which was 40 people), in the control group lost their hair just because they **thought** they were receiving chemotherapy. Basically, their intense fear of having a side effect caused their bodies to produce the side effect, even though they weren't actually having any chemotherapy (Fielding 1983). This study (and any others that I refer to) can be verified in the references listed in the suggested reading section at the back of this book.

Multiple studies show that fear keeps the body stuck in fight or flight mode, which means the body cannot switch over to resting phase. If you're feeling fear, your body can't heal – and if you are self-healing, you can't feel fear. People who have lots of fear don't produce any natural killer cells after being exposed to a stressor,

while people who by nature are not as fearful do produce them. This is why so many radical remission survivors repeatedly say that releasing fear from your body is one of the absolute best things you can do to help your body heal because fear physically reduces the ability of the immune system to perform at its best.

If you are feeling stressed about your potential to manage stress the good news is that *stress management works*. Studies have revealed that releasing negative feelings has the power to strengthen your immune system at a speedy rate. A study of breast cancer patients that took a stress management course showed improved blood results compared to a control group who did not take the course (McGregor et al. 2004).

Embracing social support is another of my favourites. Because humans are social creatures by nature, we all need each other to survive. The support of others is obviously way more important when you are sick. Researchers have recently discovered that loved ones also help to keep our bodies healthy. When we're surrounded by loved ones or even our pets, the feeling of being loved releases a flood of hormones into our bloodstream, which not only make us feel better emotionally but also strengthens our immune system significantly. Therefore, receiving love from others when we are sick actually helps the body heal itself.

Working in the caring industry I feel privileged to be able to supply non-judgemental love to those in need. I learnt this by modelling some wonderful nurses in my training. It is so much easier to tolerate the whining and grumpiness of patients when you empathise and put yourself in their position. This genuine form of caring and compassion is difficult to avoid when you really do care, however, burnout is a potentially real issue. Self-care and compassion are essential to avoid this.

No-one wants to be sick in hospital, and so a collaborative approach gives empowerment and control to the patient. I have noticed that the language of people in the sickness business is slowly changing. Elderly people from an old system and institutionalised people will comment that 'they' want me to do this (meaning medical professionals) rather than 'we' have decided to do this. Taking part in the decision-making processes is of huge benefit to the patient. It can be slower for the professionals initially, but with better long-term outcomes. That's one reason why it's no surprise to me that social support turns out to be one of the nine key factors in Turner's research. Additionally, in the book *Lost Connections: Why You're Depressed and How to Find Hope*, author Johann Hari explains this aspect beautifully.

Increasing positive emotions is another effective way to manage stress and find a happier way to live. As soon as we can get out of fight or flight mode, the body naturally begins to heal itself. You can turn up that healing by purposely trying to feel positive emotions. This is also a prevention technique, as emotions such as love, happiness and joy really ramp up the immune system.

Stress SOULutions

Whenever we feel these emotions, the glands in our brains release a surge of healing hormones into our bloodstream, things like oxytocin, serotonin, relaxin, dopamine and endorphins. These hormones instantly communicate with all the cells in our body and do things such as lower your blood pressure to a good rate, negate the stress hormone cortisol and deepen your breathing. This provides more oxygen to each of your cells and increases white and red blood cell activity, which helps the immune system to clear out any infections. It can even scan for cancer and potentially remove those cells.

All these changes have been well-documented in clinical studies, in which researchers do things like look at people's immune cells before and after showing them a comedy video. Many studies have shown that people who are battling any illness and have an overall positive attitude live much longer than people who are pessimists. Repeatedly studies are finding evidence to prove that happy people live longer and get better faster (e.g. Cohen et al. 2006).

If you feel like you are not really a 'happy person', don't despair – because it is the intention to be happy that matters. Not pretending to be happy all the time but being a genuine person with real emotions and seeking happiness even when you feel miserable – because it is healthy to be sad at times.

Rather than saying you're battling or fighting cancer, some spiritual healers suggest that you send love to your cells and create a loving energy, so the wonderful immune system cancels out the cancer. There is logic in this, as fighting war with war rarely causes peace long term. I have heard people say that they are 'dealing' with cancer which sounds more peaceful. However, whatever the individual resonates with, is the correct way.

In her book, Turner also cites a study in which two groups of men with prostate cancer (the alternative treatment group and the watchful waiting group) are very carefully monitored. In the alternative treatment group, no men had their cancer flare up and their tumour markers decreased by an average of four percent. In contrast, for those who just watched and waited, it increased by six percent.

The most impressive part is that in a follow-up study, it found that men in the alternative treatment group that had previously had a prostate cancer gene turned on, now had that gene turned off, after only three months of being on the alternative treatment regime. In other words, this study showed that by participating in the alternative program, which included lots of techniques to increase positive emotion, these cancer patients were able to turn off the genes and reduce the amount of cancer already in their bodies.

This study illustrates how strengthening the immune system by increasing your positive emotions can significantly heal your body from cancer. Obviously, it's unrealistic to feel happy all the time and the aim should be to increase your happiness. Even a small change

can be a significant step towards healing yourself. For example, you might choose to spend the 10 minutes a day that you would usually watch negative news focusing on hopeful information.

Each one of the nine key factors highlighted in the radical remission study is worth looking at, to see that you are doing the best you can in each of these areas.

WHY SHOULD WE BE INTERESTED IN THESE STUDIES?

I really like the comparison of Alexander Fleming, a scientist who chose not to ignore an anomaly, in a similar way to the people who looked for alternatives and survived cancer. His story goes that in 1928, he came back from a holiday and found mould growing in one of his many Petri dishes, however, this wasn't surprising as he had been away for some time. So, he began sterilising his dishes, figuring that he just needed to start his experiments over. Thankfully, being really observant and curious, he paused, to take a closer look and noticed that all the bacteria in one particular dish were dead. Instead of ignoring this and dismissing it as an anomaly, he chose to investigate the matter further – which then led to the discovery of penicillin!

Perhaps by studying people that recover from cancer (and not dismissing it as an anomaly) we can prevent many future cases. Although it sounds really harsh and cruel, I once heard somebody say that maybe one day cancer will only be for people who choose not to be educated on how to prevent it. I write this with love and healing as a motivator, not to cause feelings of guilt. There are still many, many wonderful people suffering unfairly despite the fact they are educated and have done all the 'right' things.

The information we have available to us these days can be extremely overwhelming, but it's very hard to ignore the potential that so many things that we choose to live with contribute to us having cancer. We need to make wise decisions and examine our priorities and be aware of all the chemicals that we put into and on our body. This does not mean that if you have cancer it is your fault only that you are a powerful human being with unlimited opportunities in this complex life.

Take for example that in the medical profession, if somebody needs some medication, we can put a little patch on their skin to deliver transdermal. The patch is like a sticker applied somewhere on the body, and it gives slow release of either strong painkillers, hormones, nicotine or other various drugs. When you think about it, every day you are putting soap, moisturiser, shampoo or makeup on your skin, and you're absorbing all of this in the same way that we deliver potent medications. Where do all these things go? It is really worth thinking about what you put on your body and what is in those deodorants, soaps, and moisturisers. You are absorbing everything the same as medicinal patches deliver, nicotine,

hormones and morphine. Think about what you put on your body. If you take care of your body, it will take care of you.

3 helpful actions to take after reading this chapter:

1. Make a list of all nine key contributors to radical remission to be sure you are doing your very best in each one. If not, make adjustments as necessary.

2. Learn more about the spontaneous and radical remission cases. Search online or use the resources from the recommended reading page at the back of the book.

3. Start or continue journaling, as it is an important part of releasing repressed emotions.

Chapter 4

Busting the Myths

'We are shaped by our thoughts; we become what we think. When the mind is pure, joy follows like a shadow that never leaves.'
Buddha

Our genes do not determine our health!

Our health is not controlled by genetics. Why is this revolutionary? Because it means you have choices about your life and your health. Feeling empowered, you can begin to improve the environment of your internal bodies, choosing what to invite, what to avoid, and what to focus on. Importantly, you have the ability to turn your gene expressions on or off. This has amazing benefits such as preventing illnesses and can also assist in curing any ailments that you have with greater skill and accuracy.

The Centre for Disease Control (CDC), has reported that genetics account for only 10% of disease with the remaining 90% owing to

environmental variables. Rudolph Tanzi, a professor of neurology at Harvard went so far as to say that only 5% of disease related mutations are full deterministic while 95% can be influenced by diet, behaviour and other environmental conditions. As he says, 'You are not simply the sum total of the genes you were born with. You're the user and the controller of your genes, the author of your biological story,' – and no prospect in self-care is more exciting.

Epigenetics is the study of changes in organisms caused by modification of gene expression rather than alteration of the genetic code itself. It has transformed the way we think about genes and genomes.

Scientist Dr Bruce Lipton defines epigenetics as 'the study of inherited changes in phenotype (appearance) or gene expression caused by mechanisms other than changes in the underlying DNA sequence'.

Epigenetics means above the genes. So first, we need to remember that our DNA blueprint never changes throughout our lifetimes. Our bodies are made up of cells, inside our cells we have nucleuses and inside the nucleus are chromosomes. Chromosomes are made up of DNA. Blueprints decide whether you'll be male or female, if you'll have brown eyes or blue eyes, what colour hair you have, etc.

We know that medicine can perform miracles. However, Dr. Lipton suggests the current protocol is to regard the physical body like a machine, in the same way a mechanic regards a car. When the parts break you replace them, transplant them, get new joints and perform other medical fixes. He believes that the major flaw of this method is that is fails to take into account that there is actually a driver in the car.

Epigenetics reveals that the vehicles – or the gene – are not responsible for the breakdown. It is the driver. Essentially, if you don't know how to drive you are going to mess up the vehicle. In basic terms we can agree that lifestyle is the key to taking care of yourself. Think well, eat well and exercise and limit the need for your body to break down and need new parts.

Dr Lipton then takes it a step further by looking at the cancer connection. He showed via scientific culture dish experiments how stem cells can be turned into any cell depending on the environment they are placed in. If cells are in a healthy environment, they are healthy, if they are in an unhealthy environment, they get sick.

THE STRESS CONNECTION

How does all this relate to stress you ask? Well your perception of any given thing at any given moment can influence your brain chemistry (where your cells reside) and determine their fate. Your thoughts and perceptions have a direct mind-blowing effect on the cells. What many of us have known since time began, but have had little evidence to back us up, is now proven. Your mind can and

does play a massive role in both the cause of illnesses and the healing of them.

Other than the mind, the other two factors that impact the fate of the cells according to Dr Lipton are toxins and trauma.

Imagine if identical twins are separated at birth. One eats healthily, has a happy life, thinks happy thoughts, has a great job, enjoys the environment, gets plenty of sunshine and has lots of fun. The other, is born into a life of poverty, takes up drugs, has a stressful job and loses a lot of loved ones. There's little doubt that the outcomes will be very different for each.

The bottom line is, that environment is the secret. Never before has it been so apparent that our environment, state of mind, cells and living abode are so influential to our health and happiness. Put your feet up, snuggle up to someone you love, eat dark chocolate, have one glass of good quality red wine, watch a comedy and you have it made! Seriously, science says so!

Most nurses have a certain sense of humour saved for times when they are in the company of others that get it. It is a coping mechanism of epic proportions. For all human beings, laughter as stress relief is undisputed. We should all do it more often.

It has also been observed that factors such as stress and diet have a profound effect on how our genetic blueprint operates. Basically, there is packaging around the DNA called methyl groups or histones and they have the ability to switch the gene on or off if it's acting in a way that it shouldn't be. Your level of stress and state of your diet directly impact this process.

Our genetic blueprint begins during early pregnancy. Yep its complicated. No organism, including human beings can live in emergency mode long-term, but sadly some people live in stress constantly. This affects their health significantly, but they are often unaware that stress is the underlying issue.

We now know that thought alone can turn the stress responses on and this can push the buttons that start genetically caused diseases. However, this reaction can also be turned off because of what we know about epigenetics.

It makes me think of a time when I was talking to my wise grandma, who was unwell at the time, and she mentioned that it was probably just 'something to do with her nerves'. When I asked her for more information, she got talking about her experiences in the war. When the bombs were going off, everyone was told to go into the underground bunkers, and she said the siren would wail and down they would go. This happened night after night. She casually described how she eventually became fed up with it so she made the decision that she would rather be bombed than to be a slave to worrying about being bombed all the time. From that time on, she decided to not even go into the bunkers, to just ignore the sirens and try her best to get on with life.

This kind of adaptation most likely affected her nervous system long-term. Ignoring the sirens may have been beneficial in the short term – but storing or denying stress has long-term implications in the manifestations of illness.

YOU ARE IN CONTROL

As recently as 1992, Dr. Bruce Lipton began looking at the principles of quantum physics and how they relate to cells and their processing symptoms. He discovered that the walls of the cells act in a similar way to a computer chip, which makes them sort of like the 'cell's equivalent of a brain'. Lipton's research revealed that the environment which operates through the membrane, controlled the behaviour and the physiology of the cell, and this was turning genes on and off. His discoveries caused a lot of controversy and he was disbelieved for a very long time, but many subsequent papers by other researchers have since validated his concept and ideas.

Having the ability to change your mindset is an incredible way of maintaining your health. When you can look at a situation and find the good in it, it is transformational for your health. This positivity changes the chemicals in your brain, making you healthier, stronger, fitter and happier. In the caring and healing environment, it's wonderful to be able to give people hope and education about changing the future of their health.

It's also vital to look at how much sunshine and movement people get and the quality of food they eat. The amount of nutritional education that the average doctor gets does not seem sufficient when you consider how important eating good food is for your health. The role of an educated doctor is often reserved for when illness hits, rather than prevention. It can be really beneficial to see an integrative GP, a naturopath, a health coach or someone who focuses more on making your life and your health extraordinary rather than just patching up the mistakes and the illnesses that come on.

But what about all the true genetic conditions such as haemophilia and cystic fibrosis? Are they changeable? No, they are not. They sit in the five or 10% of health issues that are determined solely by our genes. You can however change the comorbidities or the other conditions that may develop with your specific genetically inherited conditions.

There have been times when I've been at work caring for women having bilateral mastectomies (where both breasts are removed) and they say, 'I'm here to have an Angelina Jolie'. After genetic testing discovered that she had the BRCA gene, Jolie decided to remove both her breasts to avoid getting cancer.

When you look at research from scientists like Dr. Lipton, it's seems highly possible that a person in this situation may not have contracted cancer. The percentages that were once an educated

guess, are now thought to be a lot lower. Of course, it is also possible that those who chose to have the mastectomy made the right decision. I am not here to judge, only to try and bring more awareness. The society that we currently live in shows too little value in prevention particularly because it is hard to prove. How can someone prove they didn't get a cancer because of their behaviour? Very difficult! However, it's devastating to see people make huge decisions about their health based on recommendation without completely researching everything.

The American Cancer Society even goes so far as to say that mammography has the potential to stimulate radiation induced cancer. So, what can you do? Damned if you do, damned if you don't it seems. There is an option of ultrasound, and in America, thermal imaging which has far less radiation, or even medical resonate imaging (MRI). I urge you to do your own research, particularly if you are in a potential high-risk group.

I think society has wonderful health care for the masses, we really live in great times. If you have the time and the interest it can potentially be done even better, with some fine-tuning for each particular individual and their circumstances. If this sounds too much for you don't worry and continue what you are doing, prevention is key. In Australia we live in a wonderful First World country with great health care. My wish for you is that you know that it is possible to question and do further research which gives a sense of empowerment and often surprisingly good results. There is a huge amount of great information out there.

I read a statistic once which stated, that 40% of women have ductal carcinoma in situ (DCIS) at death. The information was gathered from car accident autopsies and showed that all these women had some type of cancer in their body but they didn't even know, and there was a chance that it was never going to go on and affect them. So, it's also worth looking at the fear factor. A lot of fear is created from the threat of potential diseases. Early intervention is important and screening has its place, however, I believe we go too far with investigations rather than focusing more on preventions. I encourage everyone to continue to get whatever screening they think is effective, as most of the tests are harmless. There is a small amount of radiation which seems counterproductive if you were never going to contract the cancer in the first place. Or on the other hand, a simple X-ray may save your life. If you were to choose not to have testing it would not be done lightly and other natural methods should be studied and considered.

Stress SOULutions

3 helpful actions to take after reading this chapter:

1. Be in control of your own health and your future health by knowing how much of a positive, significant change you can make with knowledge.

2. Being healthily happy has become so complex. Every day ask yourself what you truly value in life and whether your behaviour reflects this. Are you filling your life with things you don't need? Consider this quote from Johann Hari: *Junk food is distorting our bodies. Junk values are distorting our minds. Materialism is KFC for the soul*'.

3. Take stock of your environment, both internal and external. What news are you watching? What thoughts are you having? How are you increasing your own happiness and vibrations? Your health can be changed by allowing your subconscious brain to listen to healing meditations particularly as you are falling asleep. The app Insight Timer has hundreds for free, or they can be purchased for a small cost.

Chapter 5

The Art of Following Your Intuition

'When you reach the end of what you should know, you will be at the beginning of what you should sense.'
Kahlil Gibran

I like to think that when you learn to live by your intuition you allow the flow of life to come through your heart. For some this is connected to spirituality or strengthened by tuning into personal beliefs. This may be connected to your higher self, God, Goddess, Allah, Heavenly Father, Mother Earth, big man upstairs or another divine being that works for you.

Intuition is connected to our emotions, and we tend to traditionally hide our emotions. In our culture, women have more strongly identified with using intuition, but men are just as good at using

their intuition as women. A big issue with society at the moment is that many of us are out of touch with our emotions, and this can interfere with intuition.

Listening to and following your intuition requires commitment and self-trust. It is a new way of life which can be uncomfortable and frightening. Following your inner sense of truth takes time. You need to be compassionate with yourself. There'll be conflicted voices inside, you need to honour these voices and thank them for their concerns. The more you practice, the more success you will have. As you take small steps you will gain confidence and a secret weapon.

Your intuition always has your higher self at heart and is always protecting your higher self. There will be a little inner critic that comes out and says things like, 'don't be silly,' or 'it's not real,' or 'there's no proof,' or something similar. It is wise to just thank this attempt to protect you from humiliation and move on. To follow your intuition, you need to ask your inner wisdom, higher self, god or whomever it is for you, and follow the inner guidance. It might be nothing or it might open to a new and wonderful way to live. Our intuition is connected to our soul and our higher intelligence and is always connecting us to greater good for all concerned – not just for you but for everybody in the universe.

When you follow your intuition, you may disappoint others as you say no and follow your honourable boundaries. But in the long term, everyone is healthier and happier. Intuitive processes come from a point of balance; from a place where everyone is exactly where they're meant to be.

By using your intuition, you return to the source and connect to the universal intelligence. This is so helpful for prevention and healing. Using your intuition also helps with relieving your stress and learning how to manage your stress as you learn to operate from the heart and the soul. It's no surprise that intuition comes in as one of the top nine ways that people in the studies of *Spontaneous Remission* declare helped them to heal.

TAPPING INTO YOUR INTUITION

The Oxford Dictionary defines intuition as, 'the ability to understand something instinctively, without the need for conscious reasoning'. Some people access their intuition through prayer and may think or feel that their intuition is a message from God or the inner goddess. For me, I like to think it's my higher self being guided by spirit. Using meditation to tap into moments of clarity will also attune your intuition to be as strong as it can be.

Sometimes in my coaching clinic before I have a session with a client, we both sit down to meditate and ask a question that our intuition can answer. So that they get into the right space, I ask a question related to what the client needs to know. It's uncanny how often we both come up with similar themes such as, they need

change, or they need some work on their diet, or they need to be letting go of something, or they need to be taking action. They're generally just themes, but so often we come up with the same thing. That's not being psychic, it's just using your intuition.

There have been many times in my life when I have tapped into my intuition for what I have hoped is the good of all. Some years ago, my husband lost his job and we were forced to reconsider what we would do with our future. We looked at many different options, and one of the more exciting ideas was to go and live in another country that doesn't speak English for a year. I did lots of meditating and contemplating about it. If we chose to stay in our home, we had enough money to pay the bulk of the bills and live a more comfortable, easier life. But something in my soul reminded me that these are not the values we live by. Is there such an achievement in owning things? Or should we go out and experience the world?

When I broached this with my tolerant, adventurous husband, he said, 'it's a possibility, but we really should be sensible and pay off the bills'. So, I presented an option to him. 'How about if I can find us some free accommodation, and we can do this dream of ours within a reasonable cost?' He said, 'Yeah, yeah, sure. If you can find some free accommodation, I'll definitely consider it'. So, I sat down and visualised and meditated again and focused on tuning inwards until I found this amazing company where you can swap houses with people. I went online and eventually found somebody that wanted us to have their house, but unfortunately she only had it available for a week and that wasn't going to be enough. I played with some manifesting techniques then she unexpectantly emailed, *I have a cat that needs looking after. Could you stay on and look after her for another month or two?* I was so pleased that I'd followed my intuition and just believed and focused on what we wanted. And our time in France and Europe was spectacular.

By following this path, life was in flow. Although there has not been a lot of research conducted on intuition, there has been lots of discoveries related indirectly to intuition. This is likely because the right side of the brain is the quick, instinctual and often subconscious way of functioning.

The limbic and reptilian parts of the brain have been around since prehistoric times. This is where all our intuitive decisions come from.

The left side of the brain is the slower, analytical and conscious way of operating. It includes the neocortex, a part of the brain that has only developed post-prehistoric.

TRUST YOUR GUT FEELING

Scientists have discovered that there are over 100 million neurons inside your gut, which are the same type of cells found in your brain. This explains why people often say they have a 'gut feeling' about something. The gut has millions of neurons that can think and feel

just like the brain can. Even more interesting is the discovery that this 'second brain' in your gut can act independently of the brain, meaning that it can stop digesting food and send you intuitive pangs of warning without any input from your brain. The gut is the only organ that has this independent operating ability. What we eat effects our mood too, and this discovery has been revolutionary in treating depression. The human gut biome (the microorganisms that live in your intestinal tract) plays a much greater role than previously thought in our overall health and wellbeing. The heart is now also being studied to demonstrate if it has a similar ability too.

We feel pangs of anxiety or stress in the stomach. This may be related to intuition, because it's the body's way of saying, 'go ahead, do that,' or, 'stop what you're doing'. Knowing the difference between the two takes a bit of time.

There have been a handful of scientific studies conducted, including one where the focus was on how we make major life decisions, such as what house to buy, or what job to take. It found that trusting your intuition leads to better outcomes than trusting your logical thinking brain. In one study, there was a group of people looking to buy a car. The first group were given plenty of time to research and pour over all the information about their various choices but were later found to be satisfied with their purchase only 25% of the time. The second group of buyers who made a quick intuitive decision about their car purchases, were found to be satisfied with their purchases 60% of the time (Dijksterhuis 2006).

This is not an isolated example – there have been other research experiments conducted asking the same question. Overall the results indicate that it's best to trust your intuition when it comes to making complex life decisions, and better to use your slower, analytical brain for solving simpler everyday problems.

When following your intuition, fear may arise at the same time as an intuitive message. This can be helpful and should not be ignored. For example, if you are unhappy in your job and your intuition is telling you it's not for you, the fear is your signal to not be rash and foolhardily quit straight away. By exploring your feelings and turning it over to your intuition, something clear will emerge. Analyse away and then ultimately follow your wisdom.

THE BEAUTY OF FRACTALS

There are many ways to access your intuition, most commonly through meditation. But another one of my favourite ways is by looking at fractals. Fractals were first identified by mathematician, Benoît Mandelbrot in 1975. They are geometrical shapes that are both simple and complex. They have an irregular pattern that is repeated, so that they look the same when viewed from varying distances. Fractals can be found in mathematic equations, but also in abundance in the natural world around us. Some examples include snowflakes, clouds, raindrops, lakes, trees, coastlines – even the beautiful light that flickers through the leaves when you lie on your back on the grass and look up at a tree and see the pattern of

the glistening sunlight. Fractals tap into your visual system in a way that reduces stress and brings you to a state where you can more easily access your own intuition.

There's a physiological resonance when the fractal structure of the eye matches that of the fractal image being viewed. We find that when we look at fractals, even for a short amount of time, we get a spike in alpha wave brain activity which shows that we're in a thriving state. Brain scans have even revealed that looking at fractals can activate the para hippocampus, which is the area of the brain that helps us to process and regulate emotions.

THE BENEFITS OF LIVING INTUITIVELY

So how can you take advantage of this wonderful tool and access your intuition to improve your life? It is as simple as asking your intuition for advice and then getting out of the way. Create moments in time where you can actively listen to your intuition. It is a practice, and it can be combined with your meditation or any other activity you do to bring more peace to your life. For you this could be sitting under a tree with your pet or taking a walk in natural surrounds.

The key is to allow your inner voice a space and a place. Learn to love who and where you are, even when you really want to be someone or somewhere else. Learning to be happy in the moment and with whatever is going on will help your intuition flow. It will just come naturally if you can get yourself into that mindset.

Listening to and following your intuition will help you to identify the areas of your life where stress is a concern. There may be aspects where you can choose to decrease your stress, such as working less or putting less pressure on yourself and egotistical pursuits. Ask yourself, what do you really value in life? Seriously… is it owning a house, saving lives, maintaining good health, leaving a legacy, or maybe, living a kind and generous life? When your heart and head are in alignment and you are living by your true values, the level of stress is minimal. You know the answer deep in your heart and soul. So, are you living in your truth and your authenticity?

Interestingly, there could also be areas where you could benefit from becoming a little bit more stressed, such as taking care of your physical body. When used as a gentle discipline, stress can be a helpful way to motivate yourself.

In 2011, the World Health Organisation (WHO) announced that: 'Mental health is produced socially. The presence or absence of mental health is above all a social indicator and therefore requires social, as well as individual, solutions.'

ARE YOU DISCONNECTED?

One of the more recently identified reasons for increased stress in modern times is disconnection. In his book, *Lost Connections*,

author Johann Hari looks deeply at the reasons for depression in today's society. His own antidepressant experience and subsequent evaluation of science-based research led him to conclude that, 'the proportion of people on antidepressants who continue to be depressed is found to be between 65 and 80 percent'.

I strongly do not recommend or advise that anyone should stop taking antidepressants because of this information. However, his findings on the underlying causes of anxiety and depression are enlightening. Much of his research revolved around disconnection and reconnection, which is a growing issue in the digital world we live in today. The depth and seriousness of the situation has motivated me to focus more on connection as a path to promoting world peace.

In his book, Hari identifies nine key areas in life where many people have become disconnected. He suggests that focusing on reconnection in these aspects of life can reduce stress and depression.

The nine areas are:

- meaningful work
- other people
- meaningful values
- childhood trauma
- status and respect

The Art of Following Your Intuition

- the natural world
- a hopeful or secure future
- the real role of genes
- brain changes.

So much of this feels like common sense and natural human needs to me.

Stress, depression and anxiety have three main causes: biological, psychological and social. They are all real and none of these are related to a chemical imbalance. There is a fourth type of depression that is a chemical imbalance and requires lifelong medication. However, I am not evaluating this type here as it is not my area of interest.

While there is no doubt that a chemical imbalance is the underlying cause of depression for some, the psychological and social causes have been underestimated for too long. As Hari uncovered when he examined the full body of research outlining the success rate of antidepressants (as opposed to the selective results released to the public) it became clear that the medication is ineffective for many (including himself).

We need to move the focus from chemical imbalances to power imbalances. Sadly, the dollar does drive health research and many treatments. There is no money in advertising fresh air, sunshine,

hugs, laughter or garlic. The dollars made by chemical antidepressants is staggering. Feel grateful for the options. Place high value on the power to research and make wise, educated choices.

3 helpful actions to take after reading this chapter:

1. Before you go to sleep ask yourself a question, a deep meaningful question. Write it down or speak it into your phone and record it. Ask for an answer via your subconscious in your sleep and as soon as you wake in the morning go straight to this question and see what answer you come up with. Write it down or record it because these messages can wipe from your memory – I'm not sure why this happens but it does. Possibly the 'sensible' conscious mind overrides the less dominant wise subconscious when we are in autopilot (as we often are in life).

2. Examine your connections – work, self, family and social. Do you need to make more of an effort to connect in any of these areas? View this as both a healing and preventative exercise.

3. Decide to make at least one more positive connection today. For example, you could join or start a meet-up group, or if you notice something you admire in a stranger, be brave

The Art of Following Your Intuition

enough to tell them. You could also try connecting with the part of yourself that gives compassion, to others and yourself. If you have negative sarcasm in your inner voice, silence it for an hour or more.

Chapter 6
Utilising Energy Medicine

'If you want to find the secrets of the universe, think in terms of energy, frequency and vibration.'
Nikola Tesla

In 1928 the discovery of antibiotics changed the world forever and saved millions of people from unnecessary suffering. Today, the latest research in energy medicine and neuroscience is beginning to cause a similar shift. I have a dream that energy medicine will be utilised in mainstream healthcare during my career.

Energy medicine has arisen out of centuries of wisdom from different cultures around the world. It's easy to learn, but difficult to understand and requires some self-trust and possibly, faith in the unknown. It only takes a couple of successful experiences before you can become a regular user.

Utilising Energy Medicine

It is comparable to traditional medicine in that it is not always perfect or instant, but the huge bonus is that there are no dangerous side effects. You can be in greater control of your health immediately. It's complementary to modern medicine or stand alone. It is empowering, causes changes in perception and is potentially cost-free.

In 1992 Bruce Taino a biologist from Washington built a frequency monitor. Using the monitor, he determined a healthy person maintains a frequency of 62 to 68Hz during the day. He also found that when it drops the immune system is compromised and the lower it goes, the higher the risk and severity of illness can be. He suggested that at 58Hz we may experience cold and flu symptoms, at 52Hz glandular fever and at 42Hz cancer has an opportunity.

Everything we eat has a frequency rating. Without going into detail, it is easy to guess that fresh food is best and packaged food is almost dead. This technology may be new, but there is a definite logic to it.

There are many ways to raise your vibrations, including laughter, singing, being in nature, hugging, hanging out with people you love and that love you, sunshine, and removing electronic devices and electrical activity. Expressing gratitude is a huge one and whole books have been written about this.

Stress SOULutions

When I first started learning about energy medicine, we had some electric fences on our property, and I read that if you are about to get a cold and you touch an electric fence it can halt the progress of the infection and stop the cold. Of course, I had to try it. It seemed to work but I can't see it taking off as a form of treatment any time soon.

After an eight-year study conducted by John Hopkins University, it was found that medical error was the third highest cause of deaths in the United States. The number of deaths in one year was estimated to be more that 250,000 (Makary 2016). This is not because doctors, nurses, and medical professionals don't care or are negligent. It is because of the systems, our knowledge and also, how busy everybody is.

The skills and dedication of the vast majority of doctors and medical professionals is highly admirable, and I am incredibly grateful knowing that if I ever have an accident or a medical emergency this service is available. My intention here is not to cause fear, but merely to stimulate a thought process where the ability to heal thy self is at least considered where appropriate. By enlisting medical treatment, there is a chance of being adversely affected by the treatment. A shift in focus can potentially see you avoid this path.

HARNESSING ENERGY FOR HEALTH

In energy medicine, energy is the medicine, and it also comes from the patient you are working on. By harnessing energy or the natural life force, you can use it to cure your ills and uplift your spirit. As more research and studies on the impact of thoughts and emotions in relation to the physical body are conducted, the results continue to indicate that the body-mind-spirit system is the accurate portrait of the human being.

In a world where computers, smartphones and technology are moving at a pace faster than human evolution, we need to recognise and honour the power of our thoughts in this world we are temporarily residing in. Energetic medicine acknowledges that our thoughts are supremely powerful. These invisible energies shape the way you think and live. You affect them in every moment through the choices you make, such as the environment you live in, the food you eat, the thoughts you have, the screen time you choose and even the jewellery and clothes you wear.

There is a choice. You can go to another level and be the writer of your story as you identify and adjust accordingly the energies within you. Working in a hospital or any other area charged with pain and suffering will affect your energy, particularly if you are an empath, which many people in the caring profession are. The absorption of other people's suffering can be neutralised in part by the satisfaction and knowledge that performing a helpful service to others is

beneficial to the world. However, knowing when your energies are being drained and how to prevent this is a valuable skill that all who work in this environment need to thrive. Learning your warning signs before you burn out is key.

Many healthcare professionals and health workers of all types have learned intuitively how to do this. As the years have gone by, I have learnt this skill by trial and error. I wish I'd been taught something or anything about managing this side effect of the caring industry earlier in my career.

Although these techniques can be very personal, individualised and varied, the following information focuses on what I do and some other options I wish I'd been introduced to as a young nurse in my teens. I believe the number of early deaths and illnesses of many of my colleagues may have been decreased or prevented with more effective self-care instruction. To be able to identify the subtle signs of built up stress is not easy and highly individualised.

THE IMPORTANCE OF SELF-CARE

Part of the reason for writing this book is that I work with so many nurses that I see as real-life angels who are so run down, self-sacrificing and exhausted – and they think it's normal because everyone is the same. It's time for change. I am impressed that a lot of the younger new nurses often choose to work less than full-time to manage their stress. That is evidence of honouring health over materialism.

Self-care is thankfully now an acceptably talked about part of life. Truly wholesome food, good sleep and exercise is a basic foundation. Gentle discipline is my current favourite. It is not all hot baths and extra sleep, sometimes it is a forced swim in the ocean even though you don't want to. Or realising that being busy and taking on too much is a recipe for illness. Evidence shows that there needs to be more advancements and support in this area if we are to prevent the prediction of the WHO that depression will be the biggest cause of health issues as early as next year.

There is not one singular skill or quick fix, but a need for continued education about negative stress. Hence, this book, and chapter is dedicated to educating the everyday person about the principles of energy medicine. You can optimise your body's innate capacity to heal itself and maintain health. You can experience greater energy levels, a clearer mind and more joy to your spirit. It's taken me many years to realise that sometimes it is my soul that is tired, not my body. It's not a 10-hour sleep that I need, but an hour in the ocean, in the forest, or in the garden. Or even a few hours hanging out with a pet that shows unconditional love.

The use of pet therapy in health institutions is so simple and so clearly able to lift a person's mood. I have witnessed an introverted and reserved Vietnam veteran with PTSD be able to find that part

of them that has emotion, by connecting with a therapy dog. It is really beautiful. We don't need science to prove this, it is obvious. Like so many other forms of stress relief that are difficult to profit from, it is not as focused on as it deserves. Everyone has their own unique soul replenisher, and it's rarely just sleep alone.

Learning to manage your energies to more effectively manage negative stress, reduce anxiety and protect yourself from ailments is invaluable. You can do this by learning the language your body already speaks. I have come from being constantly unwell in one way or another (although a master of disguising my illnesses so that no-one could tell), to being generally healthy and illness free. I don't recall a flu or a bad cold for over 10 years now.

My most recent illness was three years ago, and I knew I was going to get something, but decided it was worth it. I was studying to be an assessor and trainer. I chose a course that was highly compacted into a very short time. It meant late nights and early mornings. I read my body's signs and made the decision that to get this certificate completed and out the way was worth it. I contracted a mild case of shingles, not bad enough for any down days in bed, but to me, it was all worth it. I have let other courses linger on in my life and cause long-term stress, which for me is worse than a short bout of intense stress. Everyone has a different capacity, and different trauma resilience, and the good news is that you can increase these if you know how.

ANCIENT TECHNIQUES FOR MODERN AILMENTS

Every cell in your body has incredible capabilities to respond to electrochemical signals in highly variable and complex environments. The miracle of life that keeps your heart pumping, your food digesting, and your lungs inhaling air is in part related to your energy, or your soul or spirit, depending on your beliefs. Your mind is not required for these basic functions. The beautiful complex human body can fight off infection and instinctively help us to avoid danger. However, our unevolved caveperson fight or flight patterns have not yet adapted to some areas of modern life such as long-term stress from technology and an ongoing media bombardment.

Innate skills were great when living in caveman days. However, as energy medicine revolutionary Donna Eden states, 'if we are to thrive today, we need to participate in the evolution of our body's energy patterns'. In energy medicine, it is generally believed that it is blockages which can cause illness and block healthy energy flow. Balance and harmony can be restored and maintained within your body's energy system noninvasively by EFT (emotional freedom techniques), massaging, holding specific energy points on the skin, tracing or moving your hand above your skin along specific energy pathways and targeted meditations. There are also exercises or postures which are designed to bring a feeling of calm and renewal

by using visualisations and to surround specific areas with healing energies. Try it at least three times before you dismiss it, if you are not already in tune with these ancient techniques.

Just as there are many different types of medicines available from the chemist, there are lots of different types of energy medicine. Most of these go back many years and include things such as qigong, shiatsu, acupuncture, yoga, reiki, energy kinesiology, therapeutic touch, massage and many more. Energy medicine is complimentary to other forms of medical care, but it's also a complete form of prevention in its own right. It can address physical and emotional illnesses, and it can also promote a high level of wellness and enhance peak performance. The possibilities with energy medicine are endless. In some American hospitals, energy medicine is used, and pain relief techniques have also been used in emergency departments. To my knowledge, there is currently very little of this happening in Australia, although I have read about reiki being introduced in places and also aboriginal healers, which is a great start. There is no doubt it will become more common in the future.

SELF-PROTECTION IN ACTION

To protect myself energetically within the working environment I am grateful for a uniform. It works as an anchor to my mindset. I wear specific clothes and shoes, and when I'm wearing them I have found that they emotionally put me in a different mindset. In institutions where staff wear casual clothes, I allocate certain outfits and never wear them elsewhere. I find myself more vulnerable and easily drained of energy if I break this rule and wear clothes that I usually relax in or have fun in to work. It is only subtle, but it all helps. I don't wear fragrances that I wear other places. I take a different bag to work. I have specific socks, or compression stockings for work. I generally have specific hairstyles and jewellery. And these become anchors for my mind to know right now I am protecting myself energetically. It doesn't mean that I become uncaring or lose my empathy or compassion, just that there is a part of me that is in protective mode. There have been studies done on doctors showing that a small emotional empathy part of their brain shuts down when they're at work and caring for people that are in pain, and it protects them from taking on this pain.

Other things you can do before a shift or a stressful appointment, is to go early and sit in the car or somewhere private and do a five-minute guided meditation. I choose guided because of all the distractions around me. Find a few of your favourites and keep them on your phone. I also set my intention for my shift, which may involve something such as having a calm and rewarding shift that is at an enjoyable pace. I used to worry that this meant that my colleagues would be picking up and doing all the hard work if I wasn't working hard and just having a nice, calm, cruisy day, but I've since learnt that it's not that way at all. It is through my

intention, my patients are calmer, I'm more organised and I just get in the flow at work and really enjoy my shift.

At this point I'd like to share a technique from Donna Eden, which is called the zip up self-protection. I'll explain the steps below, or you can watch her on YouTube.

In this technique, a virtual energy zip up creates a natural form of self-protection from toxins and negative energy in the environment. This can be done alone or as part of your routine of general health. It protects you from absorbing negative energies and environmental toxins. It lifts your energy and spirit and can be used with affirmations and positive imagery.

It's important to note that affirmations are most effective if in alignment with your subconscious mind – saying words that you don't believe is a potential waste of time. For example if you are feeling awful and want to have a great day but just know in your soul that it is probably impossible, it is better to say 'I am open to having a great day,' which is more realistic than 'I will have a great day,' if you really don't believe it.

So, this is how energy protection works: when you're feeling sad or vulnerable, the central meridian, which is one of the two energy pathways that governs your central nervous system, can be like a radio receiver that channels other people's negative thoughts and energies into you. It is as though you're open and exposed. So, by pulling your hands up the central meridian, this draws energy along the meridian line and zips it up. I know some people who say, 'I'm claustrophobic, that won't work for me'. If so, just try gently closing it off, like shutting the door to a room so that you have some peace. This will help you feel more confident, protected and positive about yourself. You can zip up or shut the door on the central meridian as often as you wish. By tracing it in this manner, you strengthen the meridian, and the meridian strengthens you. If you have not ever felt that other people drain you or enter your energy space this may seem a bit weird to you. If you understand this energy draining concept then experiment, I dare you, the results may give you a shock.

Another of Donna Eden's techniques begins by tapping directly beneath the clavicle bones. If you're familiar with EFT, it's the same as this. Then, you place either hand (or both) at the bottom of the trunk of your body and then slide your hand up the centre. Then, take a deep breath as you move your hand slowly straight up the centre of your body to your lower lip. Continue upward, bringing your hands past your lips and exuberantly raising them to the sky, exhaling as you do. Circle your arms back to your pelvis and repeat three times. It's easier to watch this demonstrated on a YouTube video. The details and the specifics of doing this exercise are not important. It's more about the intention and understanding that your energy is protected.

You could also try wrapping yourself in a bubble of white light or anything else that works for you. Create your own energy protection technique. Then repeat it until it becomes a habit.

So, finally, if you think it is all just hogwash and you are eye rolling and don't believe in any of this, I urge you to give it a try before you make any judgements. So, what if you try it and it doesn't work? No harm has been done.

If you would like to examine it further, there are plenty of great practitioners out there that can introduce you to it and there are numerous courses you can complete. What if you don't even believe in it? That doesn't matter. You don't need to believe in it for it to work. For example, you don't really need to believe in love but then suddenly one day you're experiencing it.

Energy medicine can also work as a diagnosis with skilled practitioners, however it's more commonly a prevention or healer and has the power to enhance other medicines. Of course, you should still go to your doctor if you have symptoms that need addressing.

3 helpful actions to take after reading this chapter:

1. Research EFT and try it if it is not already a part of your life. You could also download the Tapping Solution app which is free.

2. Create an energy protection plan which includes particular clothes to set yourself in protection mode. Also, think about your soul replenishers – what are they and have you honoured them today?

3. Download some five-minute guided meditations to your smartphone so you have them on hand to use before you enter an energy draining situation. The Insight Timer app has many free options.

Chapter 7

You Can Change Your Life With NLP

'What the most successful people know, say and do.'
David Molden & Pat Hutchinson

Neuro-linguistic programming (NLP) is a powerful set of tools and techniques for making things happen for you that anyone can choose to learn. It can increase your confidence, release your fears and help to improve your future by removing stress and illness. NLP has been used by a wide range of prominent people including Andre Agassi, Tony Blair, Barack Obama, Bill Clinton, Oprah Winfrey, Lily Allen and many others.

If you break down the name neuro-linguistic programming, it helps explain what it's all about. Neuro is referring to the brain and the nervous system. Linguistic is the verbal and the non-verbal language used to communicate. And programming is the unique way that somebody puts all this together and creates behaviour.

The facts are that we have one brain but two minds, one conscious and the other subconscious. On any given day, you begin running programs that are stored in the depths of your unconscious mind, the one that remembers how to do everything, such as breathing, walking, talking, driving a car and how to make yourself feel good or bad. This storage area (the unconscious mind) is much larger than the conscious mind. The two minds work in cooperation. An example is when you are driving along somewhere and then the next minute you realise you're already home, but you have no memory of how you got there. Your unconscious mind has taken over and you arrive home safely and park your car.

Once these programs are formed, they have the capacity for amazing consistency that produce the same results repeatedly. The thing is, some programs will work fantastically well for you, while others may have negative effects and hold you back in life. NLP is used to change the bad programs and create fantastic new ones.

In an average day for the average person, things happen and you react. NLP offers a better way. It gives you tools to react differently by choice and helps you to be more aware of your thoughts, behaviours and the way you feel. You realise what really makes you function, and you get some clarity about what you want from your work and your life. Of course, at the end of the of the day, only you

can take responsibility for your results and make changes to improve the quality of your own life.

NLP works on the knowledge that people are only able to directly perceive a small part of the world using their consciousness and awareness, and that this view of the world is filtered by experience, beliefs, values, assumptions and biological sensory systems. NLP argues that people act and feel, based on their perception of the world and how they feel about the world that they are subjectively experiencing.

It is interesting in life how two people facing the same set of circumstances can perceive the situation so differently and end up having quite amazingly opposite results. Some people just seem to be able to achieve so much more than others. Some people also tend to attract happy vibrant people, and others are good at attracting moaners and groaners. There are some who just seem to have their lives sorted out the way they want, and others who are only just surviving or struggling with frequent problems and things pulling them down.

HOW YOU THINK MATTERS

So, what makes the difference? We can't be 100% sure. There are many variables, including nervous system regulation, which does explain a lot about this. Sometimes successful people are thought of as just being lucky, but really, luck means that there's some sort of gambling involved. On closer inspection, you can see how these people don't really take chances, they are just consistent with their thought patterns.

It really is about the way you think. Taking control of your thinking is so important when evaluating your stress management and anything else in your life. The impact your thinking has on your life is huge. Some people think that circumstances beyond their control are keeping them where they are. Like a frog born in a well who thinks that a small circle of blue sky above is all there is outside the well. It's not until you get out of the well that you realise how much more there is out there. The techniques used in NLP are designed to increase your awareness, and consequently, your choices in your life.

BREAKING IT DOWN

So, you might think that NLP seems too hard to understand. But you can just take the simplest and the best bits out of it and use them for yourself. If you are unable to find the time or motivation to do this, you can find yourself a good NLP practitioner. Take your problem there and work with the practitioner to fix or improve your problem. And the great thing with NLP is, you don't even have to have a problem. It can be about creating more excellence in your life. If you don't have any time, you can go to a practitioner for fast results, and if you don't have any money, you can read about it as there are lots of self-help techniques in books and online.

Stress SOULutions

A SIMPLE BUT EFFECTIVE NLP EXERCISE

There is one technique that is really good to get you out of a negative state or if you're feeling stuck in some way. You can do this exercise in your head, but I find it's a lot more powerful to actually walk it out on the floor, so I will describe it as though you are doing it this way.

First, stand up. This is position one. You, the way you are right now in your shoes or your bare feet.

Now, in front of where you are standing, look to a spot and imagine yourself the way you would like to be. This is position two. Make it a really good, happy and positive image.

Then, step to one side. This is position three. And in this position, you can see both images one and two, which are both you. From position three, you are in touch with all the resources you need. You can go inside and see exactly what resources you need to move from position one to two. The trick is to allow your unconscious mind to gather those resources and project them to you at position one.

Just allow things to come to your mind. It doesn't matter if you think you're making them up. It's a little bit like the psychiatrists in the old days where they would hold up a picture and say, 'What do you see?'. Sometimes it helps to have a pen and a paper and just write down what comes to you, even if it seems ridiculous. You can come back to it later and decide whether it's ridiculous or not. And you'll be quite surprised at how insightful and accurate these thoughts or visions can be.

Then move back to position one and accept the resources from your higher self and integrate them fully into yourself. Then, you can move triumphantly or happily into position two feeling the way that you want to feel, seeing yourself the way you will be. And then allow yourself to really experience this.

Reorientate yourself back to the here and now, bringing with you all the good feelings you've just experienced. If you can do a meditation of some sort or a basic self-hypnosis when you are in position three, this will enhance the effectiveness. Do whatever works for you. It may be saying a prayer or calling in spirits or asking your guardian angels, whatever resonates with how you like to live your life.

When you feel under stress your mind has a wonderful capacity to put your problems behind a veil. This is to give you a sense of safety and feeling of stability in your life. Unfortunately, energy and passion also become masked behind the veil. You may create a smokescreen for your thinking, but your body is not easily deceived. Observe your body signals and the signals other people give unintentionally and use this information to adjust accordingly.

3 helpful actions to take after reading this chapter:

1. Try the technique described at least three times with an open mind. Use a partner if it seems helpful.

2. Before you begin the technique score a mark out of 10 to gauge how stressed you are about the issue and then after the technique score again to see the difference.

3. Become more aware of the physical signals your body is sending you (rate of breathing, faster or shallow heart rate, sweating, eyes darting around the room) and observe this in others also.

Chapter 8

Your Sensational Nervous System

'Our remedies oft in ourselves do lie.'
William Shakespeare

Are you aware that we as human beings have two nervous systems? If so, you are amongst the few who do. So many non-medical people are surprised to learn this basic physiological fact about the human body. We have a central nervous system and an autonomic nervous system.

Now, just bare with me here about the physiology because it's all relevant. Our central nervous system controls our voluntary activity. If you want to walk one leg in front of the other, then you use your central nervous system. You use it to speak, listen and to process and understand the written word. Our autonomic nervous system, on the other hand, controls our automatic and involuntary body

activities. So, it controls the rise and the fall of your heart rate, it controls your breathing, the tightening or the loosening of your muscles, the increase or decrease of blood flow to your skin, it dilates or constricts your pupils, and moves your blood pressure up and down.

This autonomic nervous system controls a lot of our daily activities. We don't have to think about breathing, and there's many more things that are automatic. Most body responses are controlled and regulated by your autonomic nervous system. So, it's kind of like having an amazing autopilot that monitors, regulates and alters functions in every part of the body at all times.

The nervous system controls and coordinates all the organs and structures of the human body. The autonomic nervous system has two types of nerve fibres: the sympathetic and the parasympathetic. You can kind of compare them to the action of the accelerator and brake pedal in your car. If the sympathetic nervous system (the accelerator) is turned on, it will tighten your muscles, increase blood flow to certain areas, decrease it in other areas, dilate your pupils, raise your blood pressure and increase your heart rate. On the other hand, the parasympathetic (the brake) does the opposite.

You may have heard about the rapid sympathetic response that occurs whenever danger arises. It is called the 'fight or flight' reaction. It allows our main muscle groups to work more efficiently so we can take flight or we can fight, depending on the circumstances. So, if you're crossing the street and you suddenly hear a car horn beep and you know you face imminent danger, you can leap back and the car misses you. Your heart is thumping, your blood pressure is elevated, your pupils are dilated. You've taken flight from danger. On the other hand, if your beloved child or dog has just been abducted, then as a parent you will become quite aggressive and fight for them. That's the fight response.

Obviously, it's evolutionary logic to have an extremely well-functioning fight or flight mechanism. In the old days, if a caveman saw a lion, it wouldn't be much use spending time thinking about whether this lion was going to be dangerous or not because you would likely become lion food and be removed from the gene pool. Our autonomic nervous system makes decisions without waiting for the logic of the central nervous system to make a carefully considered decision. It's very convenient because if we get injured in a battle, we will bleed less from the wound because there's less available blood in the skin. The sympathetic nerve fibres will have already shunted the blood from the skin to the muscles. It also activates our platelets to become sticky and form clots more easily. Boom - thank you physiological responses!

Unfortunately, these instinctive fight or flight reactions that arise when there is danger also produce the same physical symptoms and signs when we experience anxiety or panic. Changes are generally predictable then. The sympathetic nerves plug into the adrenal glands and the hormone adrenaline is produced. This hormone

maintains the fast heartbeat and raised blood pressures for many minutes afterwards. Adrenaline is called a sympathomimetic hormone because it mimics the action of the sympathetic nerves. You can artificially stimulate this by having a very strong cup of coffee. Within a few minutes, you can feel your heart beating and be aware that your blood pressure has risen, you may get a tremor and may also start to feel anxious and or more alert.

MANAGING YOUR SYSTEM

Unfortunately for human beings, we can even turn this on by a thought, such as when you go to see a doctor because you're worried about having high blood pressure. The minute you start talking about it and they take your blood pressure, you get white coat syndrome and your blood pressure is elevated, even though you're not moving, you're just sitting still.

The opposite to this, however, is the parasympathetic response. If you're in a state of parasympathetic predominance, you can't be anxious. The same is true when you're completely relaxed. The good news is, that you can learn to be relaxed and in parasympathetic predominance. Learning this skill is life-changing, both emotionally and physically. You can induce this response quite simply with massage, meditation, mindfulness and self-hypnosis. But generally, if you want to make a huge improvement to the rest of your life, you need to relearn and rewire the way your body works. This doesn't happen overnight. It will take time and a strong intention to make a healthy impact, but it's worth it as it prevents the worsening of conditions and halts or prevents others.

You do have the ability to rewire your nervous system and how your brain responds to stress. This can improve the health of most of your body, including your muscular, cardiovascular and reproductive systems. Your coping mechanisms will be fine-tuned, and your immunity and digestion will also be improved.

Your body is always talking to you. If you are experiencing any of the following, it may be a sign that you need to act and try something new:

- fatigue
- digestive problems
- insomnia
- immune weakness
- headaches
- high blood pressure.

Also, if you are a person who can only either go, go, go, or completely crash, it's important to realise that this is not a healthy state of being. It can lead to anxiety and depression, and is a huge indicator that learning about your nervous system will be of immense benefit to you for the rest of your life.

Stress SOULutions

Unfortunately, many people become either stuck up in the sympathetic or stuck down in the parasympathetic response. We want our system to experience stressful variables, preferably happy ones such as parties, great conversations, eating out at dinner, going on holidays and playing sport. Generally, we feel our negative stress when we're arguing, are in a near miss or a car accident, when we hear about fires, floods, relationship dramas, etc.

Nursing home clients are often not given any stressors, and their patterning and their nervous system creates drama by becoming seemingly obsessed about minor things such as too much food on their plate, a cup in the wrong place or a bowel action that's two hours late. But for the average person living in the real world with all of our new stressors such as technology, television, constantly being on the go, using all of our machinery that supposedly makes life easier, we are potentially stuck in the sympathetic response. This is not good.

Long-term exposure to toxic stress will intensify the aging process and affect memory, cognition and emotion. Stress is when the body is knocked out of homeostasis (equilibrium) and the stress response tries to return the body to its point of balance. When we learn to work at the level of the nervous system, we can learn to sense, feel and observe. And through this process, we can actually learn to change it. This increases our resilience which is a valuable tool.

IF YOU RESIST, IT WILL PERSIST

The reason I chose to learn about all this and first became interested, is because I'd lived an adventurous life as a child, and as a teenager, I was a borderline adrenaline junkie. For example, I talked my boyfriend (now husband) into doing skydiving. I was always keen to do things like bungee jumping. We scuba-dived in areas that were dangerous and with no backup boat. Luckily my boyfriend had my back and saved me on a few occasions. I also had a near-death experience when I was white water rafting in Africa. I generally functioned on high alert with high adrenaline levels, and I discovered that every moment that I was awake, my body was working extra hard just to get by and cope with all my internal stresses and anxiety. It did have an upside in that I couldn't put on weight because I was always moving quickly and always in a stressed internal environment.

However, as I got older and decided that I was no longer interested in adrenaline fuelled activities and I wanted more peace and calm in my life, I was unable to feel or experience this. I developed a further intention tremor, which meant that when I tried to do things, my hands would shake, and I noticed this was getting worse. I then developed quite high blood pressure – at one stage it was 200 over 110, which is technically in the danger zone. But because I was healthy in appearance in every other way, I was given some time to try to reduce this blood pressure. I studied and consumed herbs and

changed my lifestyle by drinking less alcohol and started a fairly half-hearted meditation practice.

After more than a year, there was still no change and I agreed to go on antihypertensive medication, which worked, and my blood pressure came down. Then I discovered nervous system work. It just felt natural that obviously my body was working overtime. It was exhausting, really. By studying nervous system health, I learnt new ways to think, but particularly new ways to move and ways to respond to my own interoception. I learnt about releasing trauma and building resiliency. I also realised that I had a certain amount of what is deemed as compassion or empathy fatigue and I needed to counteract this as well. It was an interesting process that I now enjoy teaching to others in similar situations.

The best way to understand it, is to ask yourself what your favourite stress triggers are. Is it work and deadlines? Or is it memories from the past? Maybe it's the worries about paying your bills or fighting with your children or your partner. Or is it driving in traffic?

The world we live in today is not really designed to support a low-stress life. To be traditionally successful generally means presenting a confident public face and hiding your stresses so that nobody can see. You push through your physical exhaustion and you achieve, and you try to ignore your body's stress signals so that you can keep on going and going. When did being busy become a status or a sign you are doing well? I aim for much more thinking and being time these days. This is partly related to having grown up children and making choices such as giving up television in favour of more meaningful, joyful options. Not that television is always a bad choice, just be sure you have enough replenishing activities in your day.

The absolute truth is that stress can kill us, but it doesn't have to. If you can learn to deal with stress from the absolute root cause, then you can experience profound improvement in all areas of your life. You can have more energy, focus and peace of mind. You do have the capacity to heal yourself. You can replace the old toxic ways with a new program. Today, we may not live in a world where we need to constantly assess the danger of lions attacking us in the wild, however, we have lots and lots of mini-stressors and we're just not designed to cope with that. Sometimes, if you've spent days being in a highly stressed situation, even sleep at night doesn't seem to bring you down.

As human beings, we learn to bounce back as quickly as we can from incidences. If we have a near miss in a car and we're feeling really anxious, we push all this anxiety down and we just carry on. Research shows that it would be far more beneficial if we could just somehow pull over and allow this particular incident to move through us and allow it to be, rather than resisting it. Because what you resist will persist, and these types of incidents are always stored somewhere.

Stress SOULutions

So, let's say you've just had a near miss, and it was quite scary. There was squealing of the brakes, there was a lot of danger, and although you're not physically injured, you're feeling quite emotional. And if you want to recover and not have this go on for the whole day or store somewhere in the body, it's far healthier to pull over, allow this to work through your body, talk to yourself, and use some de-stressing techniques. It is not healthy to just carry on and go, 'Yeah, I'm all right and I'm going to keep going,' because while that may seem okay in your head, it will potentially develop into long-term stored stress.

So, if you feel like crying and it's appropriate, pull over and cry. If you can feel yourself shaking, don't hide it, just let the shakes come out. Some evidence suggests it takes about eight minutes to recover, but everybody is different. Some people that don't have the capacity or the resilience may need an hour to recover. Others can just take a few minutes. Problems arise when we don't shake, we don't tremble, we don't express our pain, grief, sadness, anger or whatever it is we feel. It will come out in some other way, and probably in an unhealthy or inappropriate way. It may manifest as pain in your back or head. When we can learn how to stop and just regroup in our lives, it won't accumulate in our body. This is the start of what society considers burnout.

REGAINING CONTROL

It's possible to learn how to take control of your higher brain and become a better listener to your lower brain, which is sometimes also called the lizard brain. Then you can analyse and release stress as it hits you, so it doesn't become toxic and debilitating. The secret is to teach your brain and nervous system to know the difference between being chased by a lion and doing some public speaking, which isn't life threatening, but your body often responds to it in a way that it is. When you learn how to listen to your nervous system and this fight, flight and freeze response, you will also learn how to release that stress immediately. Then your health will change, and your wellness will reach a higher level fundamentally.

Unfortunately, learning how to release deeply held stress and rewiring your nervous system pathways to respond better to stress takes time. But that's okay. Once you're on the path and you know some minor techniques, it's just a matter of small progressions. Teaching these skills to children is beneficial for a more peaceful world. Becoming trauma informed as a society means we will understand why people react in seemingly unreasonable ways when it is possibly a response to an old trauma from a long time ago.

The built-up trauma can be accumulated over many years. From the time you were born, much of the stress you've experienced is likely stored in your body if your brain is programmed to not release this stress when it happens. Perhaps because it's embarrassing, or it's

just the way our society works. It is very complex, and I am merely introducing this life-changing concept to understanding human behaviour for you to utilise as you wish. Without wishing to generalise, there are some beautiful cultures such as the Italians and Greeks who are far better at releasing these stresses straight away. They're often more openly emotional, and it's such a positive thing. They're able to really feel the happiness and not store the bad stuff so much.

HOW TO REDUCE STRESS IN EIGHT STEPS (ADAPTED FROM IRENE LYON)

So, now I'm going to teach you a technique that has changed my life and changed the way I go about releasing stress every day. My blood pressure is now normal, and I am completely medication free. This is partly due to my improved meditation techniques, but I also accredit it to the work of Irene Lyon, Peter Levine, Bessel Van der Kolk and Kathy Kain.

Before I share the eight steps in the technique, it's important to be able to learn how to tune into your body. You may need to practice this, as you need to know whether a survival response is happening. Having the ability to quiet the mind is key, and by learning to meditate and becoming more mindful you can begin to master this skill. For the technique to be effective, you need to focus on the here and the now. You also need to allow yourself to go through the natural biological processes that your body needs to experience in order to digest and release this stress, and this includes any emotions which come up for you.

There is no real need to believe in this or know why it works - it's important to just go with your gut or your intuition as much as you can and trust the process. Even though it's very basic, it's very powerful, and this becomes evident the more you practice it. I've even heard people say it's quite boring, and I have to admit I agree! I found it quite boring to start with. But it's so simple. It's about feeling, not thinking. It's also about being able to bring yourself into your body sensations, not to push them away and ignore them. Obviously, this doesn't work when you're working in a hospital emergency situation. You must push your emotions down in those times, and there are many situations where you will also need to do that. Regardless of your profession, there will likely be times when you will need to do that in your work. Finding time to process it later (as soon as possible) is healthy. Learning to use this technique when appropriate and sharing it with children will have a positive impact on your own life and the lives of others.

So, let's practice this technique. If you're not feeling stressed right now, you can think of something that recently caused you severe stress. Go within and sense how your body and your mind may have responded to this stress and follow these eight steps.

Stress SOULutions

Step 1: The first step is to **pause**. When you feel like the stress is coming on, just stop what you're doing (only if it's safe to do so, of course).

Step 2: Next, put your focus on **feeling it**. Start noticing how stress enters your body. If you aren't sure what to pay attention to or what to feel, that's okay. Eventually you will. You need to learn how to tune into your stress so that you can respond to it and release it. I've had clients say that just by pausing and then feeling what's going on inside their body they have been able to instantly release the stress, it's all over and gone. Generally, you'll probably feel tensions in your physical body and some emotions. And that's okay. Allow your body to follow whatever it wants to do, because then you'll have the secret to coming out of stress.

If you can't do this yet because you've probably suppressed it for so long, you can just sense your physical body in relation to your surroundings. If you're standing somewhere, just notice how your feet feel in your shoes. Or if you're sitting and your back is against a chair, just feel the contact. There's no need to change anything. It's all about observing and just noticing and paying attention.

Step 3: Notice any **sensations** in your body. For example, you might be uncomfortable, and generally it's tightness which is around your shoulders, your jaw and your back. Or, if there's an increase in your heart rate or your breathing is shallower, whatever it is, just notice it. You don't need to change it yet. Just pay attention to it.

Step 4: This step is about being **self-aware**. It sounds simple, but it can be really hard. As you practice, it does become easier. Self-awareness is a largely lost skill in our world. As the experience begins to decrease, you might need to massage parts of tension. Rub your own shoulders or rub your hands together as though you're washing them with warm soapy water and look at your hands as you do this. Just look at the details of what's going on in your hands and do the same with your wrists, your elbows, your knees and your thighs. This is effective because it returns your body back to you. You're connecting and reorientating to your system, and it's going to help you understand ways to bring down this response.

Step 5: Now, just notice **your breath**. Don't change it at all. Sometimes we've been taught to take big deep breaths, and if that feels natural and right to you, that's fine. However, just be aware that when you breathe in, your heart rate goes up. If you really need to focus on anything, it's your exhalation, because when we exhale, our heart rate decreases. That's a useful skill to know, particularly if you're using fine motor skills, such as navigating, giving injections or doing anything else where you need a steady hand.

Step 6: Next, **pause again**. It's just about pausing. You gain more self-awareness and give yourself time to allow the adrenaline to come down. And just imagine what it is you want to feel. Having the intention of diffusing your stress response will increase its ability to work.

Step 7: Now come back and **engage**. Make sure your eyes are open and you see the world around you. Look closely at the beautiful trees or the plants, take a good look at the colour of things, notice how they smell. By doing this you are activating a part of your nervous system that detects your current position in the environment and you are showing it that you're safe, that there are no lions about to eat you, and that you're in reality.

Step 8: Lastly, take further notice of the **changes in your body**, such as your jaw loosening, muscles relaxing, and maybe some tension and pain being relieved. If you need to cry, cry. Think about what you do when you hold back tears after an accident or emotional upset. The mouth tightens, the throat constricts, and you're holding in all these things. So, if tears are coming, just allow them to come. Cry if you feel it will help. You don't need to hold back tears. Of course, this is only appropriate in some situations. You wouldn't release tears as a nurse working in the emergency ward or in most social situations, depending on the scene. I have cried with my patients at certain times, but this is rare. With my new knowledge I am more encouraging of tears and emotions that help to heal and provide a form of closure from an incident.

If you can learn to do the eight steps to reduce stress repeatedly through your day and throughout your life, it becomes really quick. When you first learn to do it, it can take up to 10 minutes. But everyone's different. Now, depending on the day, I maybe do it every hour, and I do it automatically now. Adjusting your posture or physiology becomes the next step. There is no right or wrong way to do it. And I know it seems very simple and it is, but it's one of the first ways to tame your survival instincts and not build up toxic stress. This was certainly a contributing factor that helped me to get off my blood pressure medication, because it stopped my body working too hard in situations where it doesn't need to.

STRESS PRODUCES MORE STRESS

Another concept to be aware of is the effect of mirror neurons. Basically, this is where we unconsciously take on the feeling of another. A mirror neuron is a neuron that fires when you observe the same action performed by another person. In other words, the neuron mirrors the behaviour of the other as though you are actually having the experience. For example, if you see someone get smacked in the head with a ball you screw up your face and say 'ouch' out loud in sympathy. Or if you see someone vomit you suddenly lose your appetite.

This occurrence has both positive and negative potential. It is possible that being around sick and unhappy people all day can bring your own shiny personality down and contribute to stress and burnout. Simply being aware of this is helpful, as is understanding that the act of caring for other people can negate the misery you witness. But be aware that watching misery on television that you can't do anything about does not have a natural way to counteract it.

The positive side to mirror neurons is that you can influence others by acting happy and smiling. Some fun experiments have been carried out in airports where whole lines of people waiting to get on a plane can be influenced to feel fear or happiness. Harvard professor and happiness expert Shawn Achor conducted a similar experiment on Oprah Winfrey's *Supersoul Conversations* to great effect. I am often asked how we can resist being overly influenced by negativity and the answer lies in building resilience and developing inner strength and inner power to be authentic. The skill of brushing things off like 'water off a duck's back' is worth seeking.

3 helpful actions to take after reading this chapter:

1. Practice the eight steps to reduce stress. First try it in a calm moment and then in a stressful situation. Keep in mind that for most people it requires about 15 attempts before it becomes second nature.
2. Listen to 'Shawn Achor: The Life-Altering Power of a Positive Mind' on Oprah's *Supersoul Conversations* for insight into how you can become happier today.
3. If you regularly watch the news or miserable TV and movies, give them up for a month and see if your happiness and sense of peace increases. Be aware of the power of mirror neurons in your life.

Chapter 9

Abundant Energy

'Wake up, be aware of who you are, what you're doing, and what you can do to prevent yourself from becoming ill.'
Maya Angelou

One significant way to gain more energy is by being aware of your internal physiology. Walking around all the time with stored up types of trauma within the body drains the energy. When you can effectively process this trauma, you can experience all the energy you were truly put on this earth to have – and with it, clearer thinking, higher immunity, increased awareness and a greater understanding of your thought processes. You will also experience more joy and fun and ultimately, a lot less stress.

In 2007, the World Health Organisation classified shift work as a probable carcinogen. In my opinion this is partly due to the stress that shift work causes and the sleep disturbances. We can be stress savvy and counteract this with the right knowledge.

UNDERSTANDING TRAUMA

If you're working or living in an environment where trauma is common, it's important to be trauma informed. One definition of trauma that I feel rings true is that it's basically nervous system dysregulation.

Another definition of trauma that was published in an article in *Psychology Today* defined it as, 'anything that's too much, too soon, or too fast for our nervous system to handle especially if we can't reach a successful resolution'.

In his book, *The Body Keeps the Score*, highly regarded trauma educator, Bessel van der Kolk describes it in this way: 'Trauma is fundamentally a disruption in our ability to be in the here and the now'.

There are three common types of trauma:

- **Shock trauma** happens when you have an unexpected experience such as a fall, car accident, dog attack, assault, verbal abuse or a broken bone.

- **Early trauma** is formed when you are a baby and while you're growing up and it may not even be very complex. We receive imprinting as a child and this type of trauma can be anything from small natural things that happened when you didn't have your needs met, to serious trauma such as abuse or neglect.

- **Continuous toxic small trauma** which are the common, everyday stressors that just build up. To effectively manage these we need to adapt, remove or increase our capacity for them.

As you can see, we have all suffered some sort of trauma, even if you've lived the best, most peaceful, calm life. It can be as simple as your needs not being met as a child, for example, if you were hungry or thirsty or had parents that didn't know how to soothe you.

Adverse Childhood Experiences (ACE) study has become a significant part of our understanding of early trauma. Its findings show that everybody, no matter how great your parents and upbringing were, suffered some kind of trauma through their childhood.

The ACE study came about in the 80s after Dr. Vincent Felitti became frustrated by the number of people dropping out of his obesity clinic, even though they were experiencing weight loss. Looking for answers, he studied the history of those who dropped out and discovered that most of them had suffered quite serious adverse childhood experiences such as drug and alcohol effected parents and major neglect.

From here, the ACE study was born, and it continues to evolve today. When you take the 10-question test, your score at the end indicates your level of childhood trauma. The higher your score, the rougher your childhood, and the higher your risk is for health problems later in life.

However, just because you've had a terrible upbringing, it doesn't mean you are necessarily going to have problems all your life. Your level of resilience is key here. The ACE study now also includes a resiliency test, to help you gain an understanding of whether this is an area you need to work on. As in the suitcase analogy, there is a healthy chance that you can either increase the size of your suitcase or slowly remove some of the baggage that you have within that suitcase to give you more capacity and therefore more resilience.

Animals have a wonderful ability to process their trauma because they don't overthink it as much as we do. There's a great YouTube wildlife video that illustrates this, which shows a polar bear's reaction after being scientifically traumatically tested in its own wild habitat. You observe the polar bear as he appears to be having some kind of seizure, but as the scientists explain, 'No, that's what animals do. They need to shake off the trauma. If he doesn't shake off the trauma, he actually has the potential to die'. It's fascinating to watch and reinforces the need to process trauma at the time it occurs if you have the option.

THE DANGER OF SUPPRESSION

After doing a bucket load of research and reading lots of scenarios about how human beings manage to heal themselves, I realised that I could work further on myself. Years ago, I developed some really intense neck and back pain all of a sudden one morning, to the point where I couldn't use my right arm. I couldn't brush my teeth and I always dropped things I was holding with my right arm. The pain was excruciating and constant. I went to the doctor and at first they thought I might have had some kind of neurological disorder. Eventually, after an MRI it was discovered I had a row of bulging and leaking disks and surgery was recommended. Many people have bulging discs and have little or no symptoms, while others who show similar X-ray results have difficulty functioning. Why is this? Well no-one really knows.

I decided to delay the surgery for a while and manage as best I could. I did start taking painkillers to function every day and had a realistic fear that I would potentially become addicted to them. I was very cautious and extremely controlled and was lucky that I didn't end up addicted like many people do. When I tried to process this trauma, I realised that one of the questions the doctors had asked me was whether I had been in an accident in my life. It was only then that I recalled a terrifyingly awful whiplash that I'd had in Africa while white water rafting.

I had denied this incident as much as possible and for as long as I could, not realising how suppression has the potential to make things worse. In this rafting accident we went over a huge waterfall called The Bad Place. The feeling of the blackness, the weight of the water and the screaming silence of being trapped under water with no way of knowing which way was up, gave me a sense of initial terror and panic, followed by surrender and acceptance. I felt the emotions of guilt for dying and leaving my children motherless, and for putting myself at risk by being selfish. I had accepted that death was imminent. Somehow, I had ended up trapped underneath the boat with my leg wrapped around a piece of rope. I remember thinking that I was going to die and that how sad it would be that I would leave everybody especially my children. I was trapped under water for so long, my body was telling me to take a breath and I knew I shouldn't. I fought and fought and eventually my head popped up and I got a huge gasp of air and then unceremoniously I was pushed back underneath the water again.

Eventually when I did come back up and found myself alive, I swam back to the boat. I swiftly took off my helmet on the swim back to the boat because it felt like there was something tightly wrapped around my neck, but I thought nothing more of it. When I got into the boat, I just had to deal with my bleeding leg and the aftermath of the trauma. I kept it fairly quiet and nobody realised how bad I was. I couldn't hold my head up, so I just rested it on the side of wherever I was or rested my chin on my hand. I also had to hide an intense substantial tremor and I could hardly hold anything with my hands. I used one hand to steady the other arm to eat. Considering we were in a Third World part of Africa and I don't like to make a fuss about anything, I didn't go to the doctors. I just carried on resting my head whenever I could. I held my heavy head with my hands and disguised it best I could. The tremor took a while to subside.

The pain wasn't actually that bad at that stage. I was probably still in a bit of shock and it was just like having a tight feeling around the back of my neck and shoulders all the time. Waking up in pain and having the weakness in my arm was over 10 years after the incident. I revisited this memory and processed it in my own way over more than a year and I believe that this has finally helped the pain to go away. Surgery was not required, and I am incredibly grateful for this.

Other times that I have had success with working with the nervous system and processing traumas is within Time Line Therapy® which I was trained in during my NLP training. I didn't really believe in it at first because it didn't do anything amazing for me initially. It was definitely working, but the most compelling proof for me was witnessed during the work with my clients.

With this technique you go back to a particular incident of your choice and go through all the details. You then think about what you would rather have happened and help yourself as though you

were in that actual incident again. When working with clients, I often write down the things they tell me as they get into a type of trance or a detached state and forget things that they say. It has the potential to be distressing for the client and new incidents may crop up, but the most satisfying part is that traumas are often released and 'lightness' is the general theme of how people describe the result. I am careful not to operate beyond the scope of my skills and almost always refer clients to someone more trauma qualified as a follow-up.

Many of my clients have experienced remarkable results, with their life improving in general and long-term symptoms disappearing completely. Processing old, new and daily events of traumas with self-compassion or whatever process is required to remove the toxic stress will in most cases, increase your energy levels. Of course, low energy may be physiological, so it's always best to have a thorough check-up and lab tests ordered from your GP, especially with any sudden onset lethargy.

WATCHING FOR THE SIGNS

The more capacity we have to be with our internal environment, to feel our sensations and notice our thoughts and then come back to be present in the body, the more resilience we create.

If I could go back to the time of my white water rafting incident, I would have treated myself with much more compassion, not worried about being such a bother and taken a lot better care of myself at the actual time of the event. So many of us have a suitcase full of stuff such as dysregulated and traumatic stress which is represented by adding things to our symbolic suitcase. During traumatic events, our body gets pulled out of awareness and goes into survival mode.

Have you ever found yourself reacting to something and wondering why? If it seems like either a pattern you repeat or a reaction that is confusing, there is a good chance that it stems from a particular past event. If you can then develop the ability to revisit and dissect this event, you can make remarkable changes. This can be done with a coach, a therapist or alone. Some fast and effective therapies do not even require telling the therapist your secrets/issues, as you play them over in your head and remove the perceived damage without reinforcing old traumas.

For many people, 'talk therapy' is ineffective and seems to intensify and rehash old issues. These days, there are so many other options you can utilise to move on from old and unhelpful stories. Everyone is different and I know of many people who benefit from and really appreciate traditional therapy. You know yourself better than anyone and if in doubt take advice from a professional. Mental health is so important and extremely personal. If you are thinking about past issues and become distressed, please do not ignore this. Either talk it over with someone trusted or visit a doctor for a referral.

Stress SOULutions

One of the more common signs that you have been pulled out of your body and are not in awareness or present with your physical feelings and thoughts is clumsiness. If you are an overthinker (as many of us are), it is easy to get lost in your thoughts. Being clumsy is one of my main signs. If I start to stub my toe, drop things, knock into walls and just generally act like a klutz, I think about what message my body is trying to tell me, particularly if it happens repetitively. Occasionally is fine, but if you're being repetitively clumsy, it often means you need to pull yourself back into your body. Do something as simple as stare at your hand, move your fingers, do everything slowly, look around and reorientate. Take a pause in time. This can be done by using the following technique, which is also used for anxiety attacks:

- Find four things you can see and say them out loud. For example, tree, roof, car, table.
- Find three things you can feel. For example, earring in your ear, wind on your face, toes wriggling in your shoe.
- Find two things you can hear. For example, an air conditioner motor, a bird singing.
- Find one thing you can either smell or taste. Essential oils are a healthy option.

When you are able to actually see, acknowledge and deal with an item, you can free up some space in your virtual suitcase. This theory that trauma is stored in our body and our nervous system is supported by many people, including doctors and psychologists such as Cathy Kane, Peter Levine and Bessel van der Kolk.

BUILDING YOUR RESILIENCE

Gaining more energy is useful when looking to culminate more spirituality, awareness and find a bigger purpose. When you accept that you are part of a team in this complicated life, and know your values, virtues and boundaries, energy flows much easier. What's more, you can cultivate social relationships that are balanced, have good communication, show gratitude and compassion.

Resilience involves behaviours, thoughts and accompanying feelings that can be developed, learnt and compassionately nurtured. It's also important to have some control over your stress response by being authentic and insightful to what's going on inside your body. To gain energy you'll need to be realistic, optimistic, hopeful, courageous, and be able to laugh at yourself. It's also imperative to have cognitive flexibility where you can reframe, redefine, and find benefits within each event that happens, and be able to develop some kind of alternate thinking. Nurses have a unique sense of humour that is difficult to relate to unless you have had similar experiences. Humour is a healthy way of diffusing stress. It can sound uncaring to someone not experiencing the same types of events regularly in their life, but in-house jokes are great stress diffusers in the right setting.

When you have these traumas that you're processing, you can be altruistic and make a gift out of your experience by sharing the stories. It is also important to keep fit and avoid adrenaline releasing activities if you're trying to heal your nervous system.

Capacity and resilience are hard to describe. They're colourless – you can't see them, but you know when they are there. For example, imagine you and a friend were in an accident. It was traumatic, but no-one died, and no-one sustained major injuries. Afterwards, if you are having nightmares and your friend has no problems, chances are you need to increase your capacity to deal with trauma.

Having a support system builds resilience – and thank goodness resilience can be learned. The more we feel all of our feelings and deal with them healthily the more resilient we are. The more in tune with our feelings and our ability to adapt, the more resilient we become. With resilience, things that would normally bother you, are now just like water off a duck's back. Of course, you can't be positive all the time, and repressed grief, anger and fear can lead to both psychological and physical problems. You can find more information on this in the books by Peter Levine, Bessel van der Kolk and other trauma informed authors.

By embracing your feelings and truly experiencing them, you develop compassion, wisdom and the inner strength that painful events can often present. Resilient people don't deny their human responses to loss and pain, they embrace them. In nursing, it's a privilege to watch births and deaths and this can be really confronting. By being in the moment and accepting the feelings you can become more resilient and resourceful. Obviously, in a work situation there are times where you have to hold your feelings in and process them later. This is really important; however, many people forget to do the processing at the end of a hard day, and this is where things have the potential to build up.

We don't need to be defined by our traumas. Sadly, with imprinting and a lack of education, many people are living a less than wonderful life. As psychologist and author Daniel Gottlieb says:

This is what happens in our hearts. The holes do not disappear, but scar tissue grows and becomes part of who we are. As our hearts become stronger and we learn that scar tissue is not so ugly after all, we accommodate what we had thought would be unendurable. And we realise that the wisdom we have gained would not have been possible without the losses we have known, even those that seemed impossible to bear.

The bottom line is that it's not about avoiding stress, it's about being prepared. You can do this by developing a strong foundation of stability through meditation, mindfulness, journaling and self-observation. Practice releasing trauma as it happens and if you think you may have old unresolved traumas, you can examine and heal this by working with an appropriate practitioner. The healing arts

are so varied and there are some wonderful modalities being developed and improved upon every day.

So, you may ask, why would we want to feel all the old bad stuff and past bad feelings and go over them again? Well, the thing is you're not just re-hashing them, you're going into them, feeling them and processing them in a way that is good and integrated and safe. This is not always simple, but if you don't process these traumas and incidents, they have the potential to store themselves somewhere else in the body physically. This can eventually develop into autoimmune diseases, cardiovascular diseases or other ailments that are particularly difficult to cure with modern medicine.

A HEALTHY PROCESS

Is it a good idea to meditate in times of high anxiety and high trauma? No, unless you are highly skilled in this area it is not recommended. Taking a deep breath actually causes the heart rate to increase which makes the overwhelmed sensations feel more intense, so instead of bringing the nervous system down, it speeds it up. When we try to avoid that discomfort by attempting to breathe it away or resist it, it may be stored away in our body for a later day. Meditation and mindfulness skills are a powerful base, and something for you to come back to at an appropriate time.

There is truth in the statement, *what you resist will persist*. As a human being you need to sit comfortably with your uncomfortable emotions otherwise, the chaotic energy gets trapped. So, if you don't address your fight or flight survival instinct, it can become stuck and left on, and then if you repress this by taking deep breaths and pushing it away, it may come back at any moment when you're not ready for it.

Repressing things is often the instinctive way to deal with everything life throws at you to avoid being overwhelmed. You may get temporary relief but then when the stresses of life compound – boom! Your roller-coaster ride begins and what you think might have been resolved comes right back. You might think you've gotten over a problem by breathing deeply and thinking about other things but there's a possibility that later it might come back and you'll experience symptoms such as troubled sleep, depression, fatigue, digestive trouble, weakened immunity, pain and possibly other odd things.

If you can befriend and learn how to be with your feelings and sensations of overwhelm, you can begin to process them in a healthy way. Depending on the situation, it may be appropriate to allow yourself to be with your intense emotion as it happens, or it may be better to repress it slightly then come back to the intense emotion when you're ready and can process it in a healthy way. But remember, if we keep resisting it will persist and eventually the flow in our body comes to a halt.

Stress SOULutions

So many of us are trying to shift and transform our ways of living and being for the better. We attempt to move away from all the bad, dangerous habits and the old emotional and physical hurts of the past which are our traumas and negative memories. It's important that we start out on this journey with solid groundwork. This involves the befriending of the uncomfortable stuff and understanding how our survival instincts, the flight and fight part of our nervous system, gets trapped in the 'on' mode and then we don't achieve what we set out to. The key to turning this around is in understanding what's going on.

When you're feeling these hard feelings, you will benefit from befriending them and not allowing them to overwhelm – and you can then discover what it takes to safely process the discomforts. This is only possible when you have a grounded base to go back to, something that you've practised and learned. And at this point, mindfulness and meditation can help you to overcome any overwhelming sensations and emotions.

The ability of food to increase energy levels is exponential. For many people removing refined food and eating mostly vegetables, quality protein, good carbs and some fruit gives the body an opportunity to heal and operate at maximum growth and repair.

When studying herbs and nutrition I experimented on myself and was astounded at the difference food makes to general health. It is incredibly complicated to find the perfect diet for each individual as we have different needs. If you seriously want more energy it is worth trialling different elimination diets where you remove something for six weeks and see how you feel. Removing dairy or gluten may seem extreme, however if you don't try it you will never know how potentially different you can feel. There are naturopaths, integrative GPs and wellness coaches that can support you in this journey if you dare.

3 helpful actions to take after reading this chapter:

1. Go online and read up on the ACE study and then complete the questionnaire and resilience test to discover your score. If appropriate, seek professional help or take steps to process your trauma.
2. Establish a good mindfulness and meditation practice and be curious about what comes up for you. Start every day by thinking of three things you are grateful for.
3. Look within to discover if you are releasing the stressful traumas of your day. For example, if someone nearly died on your shift or you had a near miss car accident, before you push it out of your mind, examine the emotions you felt and what this may have triggered from your past. It should only take about 10 minutes unless there is something unresolved. This is when you need the intelligence and knowledge of self-care to admit to yourself you could benefit from a few tips from a professional.

Chapter 10
Meditation and Mindfulness for the Soul

'If every child in the world would be taught meditation, we would eliminate violence from the world within one generation.' Dalai Lama

Meditation and mindfulness teaches people to be aware of their thoughts, so they can manage and enjoy them instead of being overwhelmed by them. Meditation is not about getting rid of our thoughts; it is about changing our relationship with them. Meditation is a way of being. For the simplicity of this chapter I will use the words meditation and mindfulness interchangeably. Practice cultivates compassion and inner wisdom.

With only a small degree of understanding, knowledge and practice of either or both meditation and mindfulness, you will experience better sleep, less stress, a stronger immune system, higher energy levels, improved memory and enhanced attention skills. Your reaction times, decision-making skills and your ability to empathise will also be improved.

Recent studies in both medicine and science have found mindfulness can positively impact our brains amazing capacity to reshape itself (neuroplasticity), our genes and their regulation (epigenetics), our telomeres (and therefore biological aging), as well as our thoughts and emotions. It is also beneficial for those who suffer depression, anxiety and addiction, or anyone wishing to improve their family life, work life, and social life.

It took us hundreds of years to learn the value of bodily hygiene and its health benefits, and now we are understanding the value of emotional hygiene for our mental health. Hence meditation and mindfulness.

The volume of meditation and mindfulness scientific experiments and research has increased exponentially over the last 20 years. A recent study conducted in the United States, found that the use of meditation in adults has tripled in the last five years (National Health Interview Summary 2017).

There is so much proof that as little as five minutes of meditation a day for eight weeks can change the brain for the better. If you stick it out for 30 minutes a day this goodness lasts for up to three years even if you don't continue it! Fifteen minutes is a realistic goal for

the average person. I find meditation a challenge and I have been practising for years. I can drop into a serene state fairly quickly now, however, I can't sit still for long. I do walking meditations and night-time hypnosis to supplement my practice.

WHAT IS MEDITATION?

Deepak Chopra defines meditation as 'the deliberate silencing of the thought process until you get to the source of thought'. He also calls it a 'mental form of yoga'. Depending on what you believe and where you source your research, there are many different meditation techniques. Here is an explanation of six of the more common forms:

- **Concentrative meditation:** For this type of meditation, you have a single focus. Focusing on the breath is the most common, or you could also choose a visual focus such as a candle or appropriate image. This can also be a type of yoga meditation or a mantra meditation, which includes transcendental meditation, (made famous by celebrities like the Beatles), where you repeat a mantra over and over again.
- **Guided visualisation:** This is probably the most popular form, especially if you're a beginner. Its benefits include increased concentration and focus. You listen to relaxing sounds and somebody may talk you through a beautiful walk or beach scene and you get to follow with your mind. Body

scans and progressive relaxation are both included in this type of meditation.

- **Open awareness:** Probably the most skilled type of meditation, this one is a little more challenging than the others. It's where everything within your attention becomes hyperaware and peaceful to the point where you melt and blend into your surroundings, although the experience will be different for everyone.
- **Observation meditation:** Here, you simply watch your busy thoughts and become the observer of them. Although you may never completely quieten your mind, provided you dedicate time and your intention is there great benefits can be had. This type of meditation is not particularly useful if you are in a negative state of mind.
- **Loving-kindness meditation:** Also known as metta meditation, the aim is to cultivate an attitude of love and kindness to all, including our perceived enemies. This can be particularly helpful in reducing frustration, anger, personal resentment and conflict.
- **Mindfulness meditation:** Mindfulness is when you have your active attention on anything and everything without judgement. This can extend your meditation to everyday life, such as when you're eating, when you're showering or doing the dishes. It doesn't have to be complicated. Once you learn how to do it and integrate it into your life, it

becomes simple. Regular practice can change your lifestyle altogether.

Other types of meditation include Yoga meditation and Chakra meditation.

THE NINE STAGES OF MEDITATION

Below, I will briefly cover the nine stages of meditation, which are more of a Buddhist explanation of understanding where you are at in your meditation practice. These stages are generally practised while sitting on a mat, but it is not necessary to do it this way – you can meditate in many ways.

Here's an overview of the nine stages:

Stage one: First, you **learn about your posture and focus attention** on an object or your breath and the way you feel it. Ensure your spine is straight and that you are calm. Hands in a mudra position or relaxed in your lap. Ensure your environment is conducive to calm. You will begin to naturally avoid distractions and learn to tell the difference between sleepy and heading into meditation. If you never get past this stage that is perfectly fine. It has been said that there are as many ways to meditate as there are human beings.

Stage two: Relates to **continuous attention**. Once you can concentrate for between one and five minutes, you are probably at stage two. You learn to be kinder to yourself, have more compassion for yourself and the world, and you have a bit more control over your mind. Your thoughts can slide away easily, like water off a duck's back.

Stage three: The third stage is **repeated attention**. This is when you are aware that you are distracted whilst you are meditating, and you learn to resettle your mind. This is when you can sit on the mat for between five to 15 minutes comfortably and walk away with a noticeable benefit.

Stage four: At this point, you are able to pay **close attention** and can sit still for about an hour of meditation. It does not have to be sitting meditation, it may be an hour of any type of meditation. In stage four, there are still feelings of excitation and drowsiness and you may experience intense mindfulness.

Stage five: At this point you are aiming for **tamed attention**. And this is also when really peaceful states of mind can be confused with a kind of calm, abiding feeling. When you become sharper and more focused, you get a deep tranquillity of your mind. This is the stage for me where it's good to join a group because you're less likely to get up and walk around and finish doing things, like getting ready for dinner or packing for the next adventure.

Stage six: The focus here is **pacified attention**. According to many, this stage is only achieved after thousands of hours of rigorous training.

Stage seven: Here, you experience **fully pacified attention** where you have the ability to recognise and pacify any thoughts and feelings.

Stage eight: In stage eight you are able to **cultivate single pointed attention.** This is where you have high levels of concentration with only a slight effort.

Stage nine: In the last stage you may achieve **attentional balance.** And this is where the meditator can now effortlessly reach absorbed concentration and can maintain it for about four hours without any interruption. In Buddhism and Hinduism it is called samadhi. For us novices, we call it Olympic level!

I don't yet have the skills to get to those upper levels. Personally, I'm not a big fan of being in group meditations. Until you get to stage five, I find that the energy of the other people in the room, which although it's lovely, is distracting. I feel focused on the other people and whether I'm affecting them or they're affecting me. But once you get to a higher stage and you are motivated to just sit there, that's when it is helpful to go to a group. It is comparable to going to the gym when you are quite fit and you're already working hard and you just need to up that level, you might do a couple of months in the gym, then you can keep going at home with whatever your normal regime is. The meditations I have described are all based on a formal sitting; however, the goal is to integrate this state of mind into your everyday existence.

WHAT ABOUT MINDFULNESS?

Mindfulness is defined as the art of attention when you are witnessing without responding. You do not change anything; you just notice and acknowledge. It's about being non-judgemental and observing everything.

It can also be described as cultivating a profound awareness of the now. It's about mastering the art of attention and witnessing what is happening without responding or trying to change anything. You simply notice and acknowledge, in a non-judgmental way. Jon Kabat-Zinn founder of the Stress Reduction Clinic and MBSR (mindfulness-based stress reduction) program admits that silencing the mind is one of the hardest things for a human being to do. It is not easy for anyone, it takes practice.

There are seven main components of the human experience: sensations, feelings, thoughts, judgements, beliefs, imagination and memory. And in our sensations, we have five senses: sight, hearing, smell, taste and touch. Problems can often start when our thoughts and feelings get confused or converge together, and then we get sensations on top of this to complicate it even more. This is where mindfulness can help.

Let's look at an example of how learning to be more mindful can help us in an everyday situation. Say you look outside and it's raining, and you can see that the clouds are grey. You can hear the

thunder; you can smell the rain. Then you may begin to feel the cold from the weather. We may feel all these things at once, plus a few drops of rain and start to feel a bit disappointed because we were going to have a picnic in the park today and now this might not happen because of the weather. So now we're using our imagination about what's going to happen in the future and imagining it's going to be disappointing, because we can't have this beautiful picnic that we planned on having. I might even imagine that I'm going to get quite cold and maybe I will get a chill because I'd forgotten to take my raincoat today.

We may believe that our sensations, feelings, images and thoughts are quite separate, but when we start to feel the rain, all of these things are combined and here begins some confusion. I might then start thinking about how I should have booked to go to a cafe and then I start to be disappointed in myself because I didn't think ahead and I didn't make this booking.

I might even feel embarrassed, sad and disappointed because I will have let down all the people that I plan to have a picnic in the park with. These feelings may then start to initiate thoughts of how disorganised I am and how I'll be letting people down. Then I'll think to myself, I shouldn't have just taken a chance and chosen this day – I should have looked ahead and checked the weather first. Then I might start to have feelings and thoughts about how I take too many chances in life. And then in my mind, I'll possibly recall previous times that this has happened in the past. So, then we have memories contributing to the experience, causing more thoughts about how irresponsible I am.

So, I've now made a judgement (that chance taking is irresponsible) and deduced a belief (that I am an irresponsible person), although I'm unlikely to realise this at the time. In reality, we know that taking chances is not irresponsible, because sometimes taking a chance is actually the only thing you can do in the unpredictability of life.

Now the combination of these new feelings, thoughts, judgements, beliefs, memory and imagination cause new sensations. And these new sensations can be quite uncomfortable, such as a tight chest, blushing in the cheeks, lumps in the throat, a dry mouth or butterflies in the tummy. When we have uncomfortable and unpleasant sensations, they tend to be related to negative thoughts. I might think that these unpleasant sensations are spoiling my ability to plan or to achieve things in life.

I might even go so far as to think there's something wrong with me and this may cause feelings of frustration and vulnerability. Then I get more images in my head and imagine being diagnosed with something unpleasant because of all these sensations I've experienced, or having a chill and a cold because I went out in the rain. And then this further confirms my thoughts that I am an irresponsible person, because I take too many chances and these thoughts become uncomfortable. Then these feelings can cause

more feelings of shame and being cross with myself and having some sort of regret and the cycle of sensations, feelings, thoughts, images and memories and judgements snowballs.

Eventually all these things will either vacate so that my thoughts do not feel connected to the initial rainstorm or all these components can come together and merge so that you become completely overwhelmed. This merging is called conflation.

During the day thoughts and feelings, even though they're separate, often converge. We don't really know when we're having a thought or a feeling because they get mixed up together. With mindfulness, it's possible to intercept all these thoughts and feelings and break them down so that you can identify what's happening and have a more realistic, enjoyable life.

HOW TO BRING MINDFULNESS TO YOUR LIFE

To experience mindfulness, you need to learn how to make space in the mind. Regular journaling can be helpful, with a focus on observation without judgement. Learning to put your attention on things that you choose and learning how to witness your own feelings and emotions without responding is important, as is developing the ability to identify those inner voices, applying self-compassion and being alert in the present moment.

Meditation and Mindfulness for the Soul

To become more mindful, all you need do is to commit to two to three minutes of meditation a day. Starting with five minutes is best, but if you really don't think you can afford five minutes, just aim for three. Seriously, we can all find three minutes a day. Set a timer and do it every day for eight weeks. And if you can find an extra three minutes at the beginning or end of the day, then that's perfect.

If you find you're getting bored, just stick with it. Before long, you will find that your creativity and ability to tune into your own thoughts will no longer be boring. So many people say that they can't meditate – well, everybody can meditate. Provided you haven't just been through a huge trauma or drama, meditating will be of benefit. In an acute state of distress, meditation can be unhelpful for the inexperienced. In this situation, other techniques are a better option, such as orientating.

If you've ever been just in the flow daydreaming or doing something that you completely love, and then lost track of time, that can be a type of meditation or self-hypnosis. So, if this has happened to you accidentally, you can do it on purpose. Sometimes in meditation you can go into such a deep thought process, it feels like you're going to the depths of the ocean. There are lots of sea creatures in the whirlpool of suppressed emotion, and they may not always be nice. So, if you think you need some additional help, seek out a qualified professional or a good meditation teacher. When you experience snippets of clarity or understanding during practice it is

possible to become so keen to experience this again that ego prevents it. My wish for you is that discovering mindful awareness will filter into your daily life and bring much peace and joy.

3 helpful actions to take after reading this chapter:

1. If you haven't already done so, download a meditation app of your choice or find a YouTube clip of a meditation that you like. There are literally thousands. Pick a theme such as confidence, stress, energy or anything that you need or interests you.

2. Complete a mindfulness-based stress reduction course (MBSR). There is a brilliant free one online called Palouse Mindfulness. They are traditionally 8-week courses and have proven to be of huge benefit in changing the brain and creating new neurons. You can find a link in the recommended reading list.

3. Invest in yourself and attend a meditation class near you and/or commit to three minutes a day of meditation practice.

Chapter 11

What Happens in Vagus

'Life doesn't get easier or more forgiving, we get stronger and more resilient.' Steve Maraboli

One of the biggest connections between the brain and the body is the vagus nerve. No, I'm not talking about a trip of alcohol-fuelled gambling disasters to Las Vegas, I'm back at the brilliant nervous system again. The understanding of the nervous system and how you can work with it, train it and make it healthier, is one of the best kept secrets to amazing health.

Vaga in Latin means 'to wander'. This nerve wanders around the body impacting our major organs. It controls all involuntary body actions such as breathing, speech, swallowing, heartbeat, blood pressure, hearing, taste, circulation, digestion, fertility and gut health. A well-toned vagus nerve will improve the body-brain communication and make your whole body more efficient.

The first time I really became interested in the vagus nerve was when I was listening to a talk by Wim Hof, who is an extreme athlete and holds the world record for immersion in an ice bath for over an hour and 20 minutes. He often talks about the vagus nerve as it has helped him develop as an elite athlete in many of his extreme areas of interests including spending extended periods in ice baths and climbing snowy mountains in freezing conditions wearing only his shorts. He's a great example of a super-fit individual with a well-toned vagus nerve. He uses his breath and cold water in extreme ways. For you and I this is not compulsory for a healthy body, thank goodness. However, his breath techniques are applicable to the general population if you care to research them.

The vagus nerve is the tenth cranial nerve that runs between the esophagus and the trachea. The benefits of learning to manage and tone your vagus nerve include experiencing more positive emotions, the ability to maintain healthy weight, improved digestion, more energy and so much more.

Individuals with low vagal tone experience more negative feelings and a higher risk of heart attack and stroke. It can actually mimic many diseases such as leaky gut syndrome and inflammatory bowel disease.

Developing your vagus nerve is like building up your muscles. When you work on them, they become stronger and when you don't, they get weaker. Learning a few simple techniques can make you feel calm, relaxed and less anxious. It can also help you feel more alert and proficient, and improve your accuracy and productivity levels.

As we evolve as human beings in this stressful world, our self-care techniques are becoming more sophisticated. You can use these techniques in every moment of every day to alleviate the effects of stress.

HOW STIMULATION HELPS

The vagus nerve controls the relaxation response through the transmitter acetylcholine. Vagal nerve stimulation therapy is a treatment that has been used since 1997 on epilepsy patients. A pacemaker-like device is surgically implanted into the chest, to stimulate the vagus nerve, which controls seizures. Every two to five minutes the device stimulates the vagus nerve, causing the diaphragm to contract. The therapy has recently even been approved in the US for the treatment of depression and was found to significantly improve the quality of life of many of the patients. The problem with the treatment is that it must be surgically implanted, it only stimulates the left nerve and it only affects a small portion of the vagus nerve.

Vagus nerve stimulation may also be achieved by what is called a vagal manoeuvre. One of these manoeuvres consists of just holding your breath for a few seconds as you do when you want to stop the

hiccups. Others include dipping your face in cold water (or splashing cold water on your face), coughing sharply or tensing your stomach muscles as if to bear down to have a bowel movement. In America patients with super ventricular tachycardia, atrial fibrillation, and other illnesses are being trained to perform these manoeuvres to keep their heart beat regular.

Studies have been done on the effects of electronic vagal stimulation, and they have shown that this little gadget induces the release of hormones such as prolactin, vasopressin and oxytocin. Oxytocin is known as the cuddle hormone. If a group of animals come together in a social context, they release a lot of oxytocin. It's also released during childbirth and during sexual activity as well as during breastfeeding. Serotonin reuptake inhibitors, that is anti-depressants, also activate oxytocin release.

So, let's think a little bit about this vagus nerve. If stimulating the vagus nerve is the key to sorting out your stress as we imagine from all the above details, I think we need to know just a little bit about where it comes from and what it does. The vagus nerve enters the brain stem. It then splits into what's called an upper root that stimulates the thalamus, which affects the cortex (the thinking part of your brain). On the lower path, it goes into the limbic system (your emotional brain).

Once again, it is worthwhile to point out that stress is a response to danger and the environment. It's the species-specific programmed reaction to threats to our survival. We need to think about the fact that all of us are feeling some sort of reaction to something in our environment that scares the hell out of us. The majority of human beings are feeling this right now, with our world in its present state and on its present trajectory. Otherwise, there wouldn't be an epidemic of stress and stress induced disease.

Our bodies are telling us something, and we need to be listening. In the meantime, we need to learn how to deal with our stress. So, back to our vagus nerve.

Both the right and the left vagus nerves descend from the brain in the carotid sheath lateral to the carotid artery. The carotid artery as you may know, is that artery on the side of your neck where you can put your fingertips, and you can feel your heartbeat there. It extends through the jugular foramen down below the head, to the neck, chest and abdomen, where it contributes to the innervation of the viscera.

So, if technical explanations aren't for you, basically it's connected directly to your gut. We have a nervous system in our gut called the enteric nervous system. It's really like a brain in our gut. We have a similar set up in the heart. The vagus nerve connects our heart, gut and brain. Although the brain in your gut functions independently from the main brain, it has as many neurons as a cat's brain. Listening to your gut is a worthwhile skill to learn. Caring for the gut is important for stress reduction. Eating good food to promote

good mood is important and worth spending time on. Understanding the connection between what you eat and how you feel is a great tool in stress management. If you learn to eat well to improve your mood, this is more than common sense and likely involves pre and probiotics.

By stimulating the vagus nerve, you can affect the high root from the thalamus to the cortex. When you affect the cortex in this way, you produce what is called sensory motor rhythm, or SMR. This is an activated pattern in the parietal cortex that is associated with the state of relaxed vigilance. In other words, it makes you very aware and very alert, but at the same time, you are relaxed and not stressed. Animals or humans exhibiting SMR show improved sleep, digestion, thinking and memory. It's also been said that learning to control this SMR state prevents you from craving drugs and overeating. It is possible to achieve all these benefits by self-stimulation of the vagus nerve through controlled breathing exercises.

IT'S ALL IN THE BREATH

Remember, the left and right vagus nerves pass between the trachea and the esophagus. Breath training that induces stimulation of the vagus nerves reduces sympathetic nervous system over-arousal. It increases parasympathetic nervous system activity, which is the relax, recuperate and regenerate system. This calms you down. The important thing to note here is that the beneficial effects of controlled breathing on the vagus nerve occur primarily during exhalation. During exhaling, your heart rate decelerates and during the period of deceleration of the heart, the vagus becomes active. Shallow, rapid breathing patterns inhibit the vagus, because the period of vagal activity is too short. By slowing down your breathing, you create more vagal activity, accentuating its relaxing and regenerating effects.

Not only is breath the engine of the sounds we make, deep inhalations and exhalations are inextricably linked with emotionality and altered states. To the Chinese, breath had the metaphorical importance that we give to blood. To them, breath was life. To breathe was to be. And to breathe deeply, was to move your Chi – which was considered to be the energy of your soul.

Because anyone at any time can be overrun by physiological stress, the level of toxicity in stress becomes so high that we need to evolve as humans and adapt and thrive.

In the book, *The Body Keeps the Score*, author Dr Bessel van der Kolk explains how 80% of the fibres of the vagus nerve which connect the brain with many internal organs, run through the body to the brain and alerts us to change. This means we can directly train our arousal system by the way we breathe, chant and move. This is a principle that has been utilised for centuries, in China, India and by every religious practice that we know of, but it's not yet accepted in the mainstream culture that we currently live in.

It's been shown that just 10 weeks of yoga can decrease PTSD symptoms, particularly if people did not respond to medication or any other treatment. When you learn how to breathe calmly, effectively and remain in a state of physical relaxation, you have an essential tool for stress management. Slow, deep breaths put the brake on the parasympathetic nerves and your arousal. However, it is important to be aware that it is the outbreath that decreases the heart rate. This is a useful tip when you need to do something that requires a steady hand. I use this when I need to give injections or take blood. You are essentially tricking your brain into thinking, 'you got this'. Another quick tip is to chew gum. The stress response causes the mouth to become dry, therefore if you chew gum and produce saliva, the brain becomes partly confused and thinks there is less stress happening. This is great for short-term problems only.

If you think this is all too complicated, and there's just too much science and pathophysiology, then don't worry about it. You can just do the exercises and you'll get the benefits whether you understand why they're happening and why they're working or not. You will discover over time, little by little, just by applying some of these basic nervous toning skills on the vagus nerve, your lifestyle and quality of life will improve.

THE STATE OF YOUR VAGUS

So, how do you even know if you have vagus nerve problems? It's the largest cranial nerve and it passes through multiple vital organs, and when the nerve is damaged these organs cannot receive the signals and information your body is sending. You'll notice localised symptoms of organ dysfunction, which doesn't mean that your organs will stop working, but some of them will work less.

One of the main functions of the vagus nerve is to supply sensation to the muscles of the vocal cord, and it can interfere with your voice and your breathing. Other muscles that are supported by the vagus nerve will be as affected as well. A lot of people think that a low amount of electrolytes like magnesium and potassium is the cause of your muscle cramps. But the cause may actually be damage to your vagus nerve. You may feel a dull kind of pain at the back of your head, which makes it not all that easy to diagnose, however toning the vagus nerve may help.

One of the more serious symptoms is fainting, which happens when you're nervous, overactive, and overstimulated. You experience sudden episodes of fainting and collapse. Other symptoms are peptic ulcers and generalised gastrointestinal disorders.

One of the most effective ways to promote a healthy vagus nerve is to learn how to do correct breathing. It sounds obvious, but many of us do not breathe the way we should. This is in part due to the

idea in today's society that a flat stomach is preferable. This has led to people training themselves to breathe incorrectly, almost reversely. When you breathe in, your lungs should inflate and your stomach should rise, and as you breathe out, your stomach should go down.

There are other simple things you can do. One of the most important and fastest ways to stimulate your vagus nerve is by having a cold shower. Splashing cold water on your face is effective too, especially as a type of emotional first aid. It is interesting that some people do this naturally without understanding the physiology behind it – this is our natural instincts at their best.

Singing is also great because it uses your voice box. Other everyday techniques include chanting, meditation, yoga, laughing, breathing exercises, fasting, Tai Chi, sleeping on your right side, chewing on gum, tensing the stomach muscles, gargling and nurturing positive social relationships.

When you learn how to breathe effectively and remain in a state of physical relaxation, you have an essential tool for stress management. The breath is another complete topic that I would recommend exploring. It can be used to induce sleep, reduce pain, bring you back to being mindful and be used as first aid for your uncontrolled emotions.

3 helpful steps to take after reading this chapter:

1. Watch or read anything by vagus nerve expert Dr Stephen Porges, who established the polyvagal theory.

2. Learn to breath correctly and gargle daily – it tones the vagus nerve.

3. Integrate cold submersion into your daily routine. Personally, I struggle with the cold, so I found it really, really horrible to start with! A cold shower or swim is a great time to psych yourself up to get any negative emotions such as anger or fear out of your system. Remember gentle discipline is good for you. I have been known to be repeatedly swearing and muttering whilst freezing in a cold shower, 'I hate this bloody cold water' over and over. When descending into a low state for no apparent reason, try this technique. Reliable state breaker every time and a nerve toner – bonus! It just depends which pain you prefer. This is great for preventing low moods from taking hold.

Chapter 12

The Magic of Intention

'Imagination is more important than knowledge. For knowledge is limited, whereas imagination embraces the entire world, stimulating progress, giving birth to evolution.' Albert Einstein

We are spiritual beings with infinite potential and when life seems like drudgery, (yep, we've all been there) the gratitude is in knowing that we can create more adventures and find inspiration in the possible.

Understanding the value of deciding what you intend or want to incur is life-changing. You can find hope where there was none, and you have a huge input into creating your future rather than just being swept along. Harnessing your intention can be improved with practice, and it has the ability to assist your healing. It is calming and stress-relieving because you can expand and see the possibilities.

The Magic of Intention

'It's not about the goal, it's about how you feel when you get there.'
Danielle LaPorte

An intention differs from a goal. It's broader, it's bigger, it's not specific, not measurable, and not often time-associated, whereas a goal is ideally specific, measurable, time-orientated and realistic. Intentions are not concrete the way goals are. They are thoughts about who and what, we want and need to be.

An article in *Psychology Today* stated that 'visualisation is a cognitive tool accessing imagination to realise all aspects of an object, action or outcome. This may include recreating a mental sensory experience of sound, sight, smell, taste and touch'.

Brain studies now reveal that thoughts produce the same mental instruction as actions. Mental imagery impacts many cognitive processes in the brain – motor control, attention, perception, planning and memory – so the brain is getting trained for actual performance during visualisation.

So, why bother? Without intention, you are giving permission to the universe to just allow, 'whatever happens to happen' and you need to make peace with this, if that is your choice. But by just sitting down and spending 10 minutes a day using self-hypnotic relaxation techniques, you can reduce your anxiety levels and bring your adrenalin levels back to normal. And why not utilise the increased access to your unconscious that you have in this state? It

will help you stay calm and achieve greater feelings of self-confidence and wellbeing. Going into a trance and not using it to give yourself positive suggestions is a bit like going for a drive in a car without a destination.

It's probably worth understanding the different brain states that can be measured in our brains using an EEG. I believe it is as follows.

Gamma waves are at their fastest, highest frequency and fire in the brain when we are learning something new, processing or perceiving messages (38–42 Hz). They promote neuroplasticity and accompany sharp insights. There are many binaural beat tracks that you can listen to online, that produce interesting effects. If you have no experience with this try it and see what it does for you.

Beta state (which is 12–38 Hz), is your everyday state. It's when you're alert, you're completely tedious, and it's how you generally go about your day.

Then there's the **alpha state** which we move into for meditation and sometimes in self-hypnosis (8 to 12 Hz). You're relaxed, and yet you're awake. It's a great gateway to the subconscious mind and useful if you want to utilise some helpful affirmations (remember, affirmations are most effective if you can believe them).

Then there's the **theta state** (3–8 HZ) and that's quite a slow brain. It's the deep relaxation, just before sleep. It's also really good for implanting suggestions and if you can get to that state in hypnosis or if you can have something that you have listened to beforehand and then listen to it as you go into sleep, it can produce profound changes, especially when done over a 21-night period. This is the frequency that is known to improve and aid our intuition.

Interestingly, I overheard a group of patients waking up in the recovery bay after various minor operations and all saying that they had just had some great dreams. The anaesthetist informed them that it was because she hypnotised them as they were being induced into an anaesthetic. A traditional type of anaesthesia with perhaps a suggested intention during their final moment of consciousness. How wonderful.

Then there are **delta waves** (0–3 Hz) and that's completely deep sleep. These waves are associated with restorative sleep and are found mostly in babies and young children as we produce less of them as we age.

KNOWING VS. THINKING

Bringing intentions and dreams into reality requires both good quality goal setting and the ability to listen to your intuition. The way life delivers on our intents and desires is often through intuitive communications that give us clarity on which paths to take and gentle nudges that help us make decisions on what to do or what not to do. We receive these communications all the time and they often go unrecognised or misunderstood. We take them for granted

and explain them away, resist and suppress them, and sadly they often stop trying to help.

If you want to become more open to, or sensitive to these messages from within, it's possible when you choose to listen and practise.

I love this example from Greek mythology. It tells the story of when King Hiero from Sicily, wanted a gold crown to offer his gods. He gave the goldsmith the gold and waited for his crown. But when he receives the crown, he suspects that that the goldsmith might have cheated him by replacing some of the gold with an inferior metal. This often happened in those days a long, long time ago.

King Hiero asked his scientist and philosopher, Archimedes, to come up with a way to assess the crown's purity. The legend goes that as Archimedes pondered how to solve this problem, he ran ideas through his mind and kept on thinking as he pondered, then eventually he decided to have a bath. As he stepped into the bath the water increased and he realised the volume of displaced water must be equal to the volume of the part of his body that's submerged. This realisation inspired his solution to the question of the crown's purity.

First, he would place the crown on a tub and measure the displaced water, and then he would put a lump of pure gold in and measure it again. And if the crown consisted of pure gold, the amount of displaced water would be equal in both cases. The story goes that once this idea hit Archimedes, he got so excited that he jumped out of the bath and ran through the streets naked yelling, 'Eureka!' which is Greek for 'I found it'. At the time, the locals obviously thought he'd gone out of his mind, which, technically, he had. He'd had a flash of clarity and insight by going 'out of his mind', so to speak.

It's common to have these sudden realisations. I think everybody has them whether you're tuned into your intuition or not. They can be called aha moments, eureka moments or epiphanies and they often occur when you're in the bath, the shower, the garden, in nature or at other times when you're in flow and in touch with your own thoughts. When these thoughts flow into our conscious mind, we feel enthusiasm, relief, gratefulness and happiness, and wonder why we hadn't come to this realisation earlier.

The above story illustrates the difference between thinking and knowing. Thinking occurs as an electric chemical process in the brain. It's predominantly rational and contemplates the pros and cons and the why and the why not of a situation. In contrast, knowing (such as an aha moment) is different to intellect because it's often accepted as intuition which can be defined as immediate realisation without the conscious state, or conscious use of reasoning. It's not a logical process to reach a sensible outcome. Rather, it's like, boom, or eureka, and we suddenly get it.

These aha moments are beautiful illuminations of clarity and enthusiasm – and when you have a clear intent or issue in mind, it has the potential to be achieved or solved within these moments of flow. Unfortunately, these moments are often squashed because our intuition is fighting our intellect. The intellect and many of the thoughts we think are only justifications produced by the cortex level of our brain as a reactive explanation for triggered emotional impulses, and much of this has been imprinted as we formed our thought processes as children.

Much research proves this. It's the old zero-to-seven-years-old basis of our behaviours and thoughts that is prolific through psychology manuals. Our current thoughts are often inaccurate interpretations of the circumstances and facts of a past situation. The past experiences are clouded by emotion, whereas intuition is a new and different source of awareness with a greater overview and possibly, a spiritual impact.

Most of us have had experiences of intuition versus intellect. But sadly, it's not widely accepted in our culture to follow our intuition at all. This is particularly evident in the school system where results from the left brain such as your intellectual, analytical and logical side are emphasised and rewarded.

As Albert Einstein said, 'The intuitive mind is a sacred gift and the rational mind is a faithful servant. We have created a society that honours the servant and has forgotten the gift'.

READY TO GO OUT OF YOUR MIND?

In modern times, the world is coming to appreciate the creative side and the right side of our brains a lot more. We are beginning to recognise its potential to improve our quality of life and our ability to be higher beings that care for the good of the world. To become masters of our destiny and to be able to harness the magic of intention, we need to, in a way, 'go out of our minds' and tune in to our higher consciousness. When learning the skill, it may seem a little bit crazy, but it can be done constructively. These intuitions that often become our intentions come to us, in many ways, disguised as inspiration, flashes of clarity, having an epiphany, gut feelings, hunches, etc.

As I mentioned above, they often come to us when we're going about our routine activities. This could be during exercise, while watching a movie, cleaning the house, painting, looking at art, staring at sunsets, during prayer and in many other situations. These moments of clarity can pop into our mind at any time, but unless you allow yourself to tune into them, they'll be pushed away as nonsense.

One way to improve our chances of taking notice of our intuition is to set an intention (or goal if you prefer) for the day. But what about those days that you don't really want to have a goal, you want to just chill out? Unfortunately, because of the way that our minds, bodies and life patterns form, this may turn out to be the day that, for

example, you fall over and injure your ankle. So instead, you could try saying something like, 'I choose to have a day where I recharge my batteries, tune into my intuition and finish a book,' then your mind has a path to travel and won't just throw things at you and create things that you may not enjoy. That also follows the pattern of what's happened in your past. To remove negative dramas in your life, set intentions of what you actually want. Remove the dramas in your life and invite in more blessings and even miracles. This can be life-changing, but it does take some perseverance.

Unfortunately, any research done on this kind of thing is difficult to prove. It's really hard to prove consciousness. However, Professor William A. Tiller has discovered some evidence that subtle energy fields respond to human intention. This can be explored further in Donna Eden's book, *Energy Medicine* and the idea also features in the movie *What the Bleep Do We Know!?*.

There have been many experiments conducted about the power of visualisations to enhance motor skills and performance, particularly in sport. A famous study conducted by Australian psychologist Alan Richardson back in 1967 involved three groups of basketball players. One group physically practised taking free throws, the next performed compelling visualisations of themselves making the shot and the last group did nothing. The group who practised, improved their shooting by 24% and the group who did nothing (unsurprisingly) showed no improvement. Interestingly, the group who performed visualisations, improved their free throw accuracy

The Magic of Intention

by 23% – almost as much as those who physically practised (Richardson 1967).

The Australian Institute of Sport (AIS) also uses visualisation techniques to teach athletes to become better at their sports. Known as 'high performance mental skills' it is a technique used by many who play sport, particularly elite athletes. You can see examples when you watch certain athletes and learn about their behaviour. They mentally rehearse before making an important move, using the technique both in preparation and during competition.

Maybe you think it's all just a bit airy-fairy and you don't really believe in any of it. I can understand why you think this if you have not had any supporting experiences. My advice is: start small. In the past it has been difficult to prove the effectiveness of 'unconventional' techniques. However, now there are so many studies being done on things like meditation and mindfulness, backed up by scientific evidence such as photographs of the brain and how it has changed, giving us conclusive proof that these things are all real and science based.

Many years ago, I met an elderly aboriginal woman who had lived off the land all her life and had minimal contact with white people. Her English was reasonable, and she stunned me by saying, 'I don't believe in germs'. She was difficult to convince, however aren't we just the same with some of our illness and energy beliefs?

Maybe you are thinking, 'It's not even worth doing positive thinking because it sounds like it's not effective sometimes'. Positive thinking and setting intentions and goals are definitely worth doing. Like most things in life it takes effort and practice, and there can be a few catches. But if you take the time to learn the techniques and understand how to get around any potential roadblocks, then your success rate will be increased exponentially.

PUT IT INTO PRACTICE

One technique you can use to harness the magic of intention is learning some self-hypnosis, focusing on a list of suggestions of things that you want to change.

Here is one simple way to bring yourself into self-hypnosis:

- Find a point somewhere to stare at (it doesn't have to be anything special)
- While you're staring at this spot (not ever losing focus), become aware of your peripheral vision
- Do the five, four, three, two, one technique where you focus on five things you can see, four things you can hear, three things you can smell, two you can touch and one you can taste.

An effective technique to try is, while staring at a point, focus on your peripheral vision without moving your eyeballs. You possibly

The Magic of Intention

do this and do not even acknowledge what you are doing. If you catch yourself doing this try immediately making a suggestion to yourself as reality comes back, such as, 'I am feeling calm and energetic,' or 'every day in every way I am getting better and better,' or 'I am going to complete this day with joy and efficiency,' or anything else that works for you.

The other action that is life-changing is setting your intention at the beginning of every day and taking note of how your life changes. This is a lot more effective if you actually write down your intentions thanks to the mind-hand-eye coordination required to put pen to paper. By setting and recording your intentions they're more likely to happen, and this is true for most people. Another simple but effective technique is to learn how to tune into your intuition more. When you have these aha moments, tune in and listen to them and see what inspiration you feel.

Our ability as a human race to experience and triumph over stress is in part a cultural issue. We are conditioned by our past experiences. We are so privileged with opportunities because of the recent discoveries in neuroscience. You cannot unknow all of this information. The fact that we can choose to step into the magic, whilst embracing also the sadness and pain is a beautiful part of being human.

As you experience this very moment in time, I want you to contemplate the fact that over the last two million years the human

brain has continued to develop the prefrontal cortex into its most evolved state ever. It is not fully evolved until age 25 according to research. This is the part of the brain that has allowed us to develop the skill of being able to imagine something before it happens. It is our peace tool.

As we learn to master this skill, we also have the power to change our own future. The degree to which we can do this remains unknown at this time. If you have this knowledge and awareness please use your magnificent power for the good of all humanity, especially yourself. You are probably already doing it to a certain level. Ramp it up. Have fun with it.

Relax into the knowing that as you accept the things you cannot change you will change into a more peaceful being. Congratulate yourself for having courage in those moments that you are brave and change for the better. Set a goal to connect with your own wisdom. Imagine great things, perform kind deeds and live a joyful authentic life.

3 helpful actions to take after reading this chapter:

1. Try listening to a binaural track for something specific such as pain relief or weight loss. There are many options online.

2. Get yourself a journal or notebook and write down your daily intentions. Note any interesting developments in your day that may have stemmed from this. Write down any aha moments you have throughout the day too.

3. Try some mental rehearsal performance techniques such as visualisation as elite athletes do and test its effectiveness.

References and Recommended Reading List

Achor, S 2015, 'The life-altering power of a positive mind', *Oprah's Supersoul Conversations*, aired 13 October, season 1, ep. 106, <http://www.oprah.com/own-supersoulsessions/shawn-achor-the-life-altering-power-of-a-positive-mind-video>.

Braunschneider, Heidi 2013, 'Preventing and managing compassion fatigue and burnout in nursing', *ESSAI*, vol. 11, article 11, <http://dc.cod.edu/essai/vol11/iss1/11>.

Chopra, Deepak & Tanzi, Rudolph E 2017 *The healing self: supercharge your immune system and stay well for life*, Ebury Publishing, London.

Cohen, S, Alper, CM, Doyle, WJ, Treanor, JJ & Turner, RB 2006, 'Positive emotional style predicts resistance to illness after experimental exposure to rhinovirus or influenza a virus', *Psychosomatic Medicine,* Nov-Dec, 68(6), pp. 809-15.

Dijksterhuis, A 2006, 'Think different: the merits of unconscious thought in preference development and decision making', *Journal of Personality and Social Psychology,* November, 87(5), pp. 586-98.

Eden, Donna & Feinstein, John 2008, *Energy medicine: how to use your body's energies for optimal health,* Little Brown Book Group, London.

Gilbert, Dan 2004, 'The surprising science of happiness', *TED talk,* February, <https://www.ted.com/talks/dan_gilbert_asks_why_are_we_happy?language=en>.

Fielding, J.W et al. 1983, 'An interim report of a prospective, randomised, controlled study of adjuvant chemotherapy in operable gastric cancer: British Stomach Cancer Group', *World Journal of Surgery* May, 7(3), pp. 390-9.

Hari, Johann 2018, *Lost connections: uncovering the real causes of depression – and the unexpected solutions,* Bloomsbury, London.

Insight Timer, <https://insighttimer.com>.

Jamieson, JP, Nock, K & Mendes, WB 2012, 'Mind over matter: reappraising arousal improves cardiovascular and cognitive responses to stress', *Journal of Experimental Psychology*, August, 141(3), pp. 417-422.

Kabat-Zinn, Jon 1994, *Wherever you go, there you are*, Piatkus, London.

Keller, A, Litzelman, K, Wisk, LE, Maddox, T, Cheng, ER, Cresswell, PD & Witt, WP 2012, 'Does the perception that stress affects health matter? The association with health and mortality', *Health Psychology*, September, 31(5), pp. 677-84.

Kolk, Bessel van der 2014, *The body keeps the score: brain, mind and body in the transformation of trauma*, Penguin, London.

Levine, Peter A 1997, *Waking the tiger: healing trauma*, North Atlantic Books, Berkeley, CA.

Lipton, Bruce H 2005, *The biology of belief*, Mountain of Love, San Francisco.

Lyon, Irene 'Tune up your nervous system' online course, <https//irenelyon.com>.

References and Recommended Reading List

Makary, MA & Daniel, M 2016, 'The third leading cause of death in the United States', *The BMJ*, published online 3 May, <https://www.bmj.com/content/353/bmj.i2139>.

Mate, Gabor 2003, *When the body says no: the cost of hidden stress*, Scribe Publications, Carlton North.

McGonigal, Kelly 2013, 'How to make stress your friend', *TED Talk*, June, <https://www.ted.com/talks/kelly_mcgonigal_how_to_make_stress_your_friend?language=en>.

McGregor, BA, Antoni, MH, Boyers, A, Alferi, SM, Blomberg, BB & Carver, CS 2004, 'Cognitive-behavioural stress management increases benefit finding and immune function among women with early-stage breast cancer', *Journal of Psychosomatic Research*, January, 56(1), pp. 1-8.

Moulden, David & Hutchinson, Pat 2006 *Brilliant NLP: what the most successful people know, say and do*, Pearson Education, Harlow.

Pezzullo, L 2019, *The cost of pain in Australia*, published online 4 April, <https://www.painaustralia.org.au/>.

'Palouse mindfulness: mindfulness-based stress reduction', free online MBSR training course, <https://palousemindfulness.com/>.

Perry, L, Gallagher, R & Duffield, C 2015, 'The health and health behaviours of Australian metropolitan nurses: an exploratory study', *BMC Nursing*, published online 3 September, <https://www.ncbi.nlm.nih.gov/pmc/articles/PMC4558723/>.

Porges, Stephen W 2004, *The polyvagal theory: the transformative power of feeling safe*, WW Norton & Co, New York.

Richardson, A 1967, 'Mental practice: a review & discussion Parts 1 & 2', *Research Quarterly*, vol. 38, iss. 1.

Schneider, Jennifer P 2004, *Living with chronic pain*, Hatherleigh Press, New York.

Turner, Kelly A 2014, *Radical remission: surviving cancer against all odds*, Harper Collins, New York.

Weil, Andrew 1995, *Spontaneous healing*, Random House, New York.

About the Author

Niomi Reardon has been a registered nurse for over 30 years. She works as a relieving nurse in all areas, and as a life coach, utilising NLP techniques. She has studied natural medicine and has a strong connection to the earth. Niomi has always known her purpose was to help other people, shown in her strong desire to help ease suffering from an early age. She was blessed to grow up with a loving, adventurous family and now enjoys exploring and embarking on more adventures with her husband and three daughters.

After reaching a stage in her career where she was frequently stressed and unwell, Niomi embarked on a mission to find optimum health and be medication free. She is now passionate about sharing this information with you.

She found that after many years of shift work and caring for the sick and injured, that she experienced a type of burnout. Dragging herself out of bed every day became normal. As her levels of empathy decreased and her ailments increased, she discovered the techniques shown in this book and began to reverse this. She likened herself to a duck gliding serenely on a pond, looking peaceful and in control, however beneath the water the little webbed feet were flailing around and aching from trying to keep up and survive.

Through her own experiences learning effective stress management techniques, and those of her patients and clients, she realised that being in a constant state of stress had become normal for most people. 'The nervous system we have was designed for the beginning of evolution and has not adapted to modern living. We must now be much kinder to ourselves and others to experience a more beautiful life,' she says.

Niomi takes great joy in teaching others life-changing skills to prevent, improve and remove the effects of negative stress. Acknowledgment of the mind body connection is taking longer in general society than she expected, and it is her mission to help others see the possibilities and utilise the many simple techniques available to promote peace and happiness.

She currently lives happily on a piece of paradise in the Adelaide Hills on acreage with her family and pets. Niomi is a vegetarian for

About the Author

ethical and environmental reasons. Her hobbies include overnight hiking, drinking shiraz with good company, dogs, reading, natural medicine and travelling. She is grateful every day for the luck she has been dealt in this lifetime.

To learn more and expand on this information:

Head to my website: http://www.lifesoulcoaching.com.au

Join my Facebook group: Stress SOULutions

Offer 1

Stress Soulutions Seminars and Workshops for Business

Would you like to show your team how to **not just manage stress but master it?**

Through seminars and workshops tailored to the needs and messaging of your organisation, I'll help those who work with you to **present the best version of themselves to your clients and stakeholders** – and to reach their full potential at work and in life.

Topics covered include:

- **Healthy relaxed living:** Explores the undisputable connection between stress and illness and how you can achieve ultimate health throughout your life.

- **Thank your pain:** Learn the language that our bodies speak so you can understand and interpret the messages and act early to stay well.
- **Feel good formula:** Understanding the science behind cancer prevention. This could save your life.
- **Busting the myths:** Your genes do not determine your health. So, now you know… what next? Learn to utilise neuroscience and accelerate your strengths.
- **The art of following your intuition:** The most powerful person in your life is you. Learn simple but powerful techniques to harness this.
- **Utilising energy medicine:** Combining old and new knowledge, to determine what is best for you.
- **Change your life with NLP:** Neurolinguistic programming can be simple, fun and life-changing.
- **Your sensational nervous system:** When you learn how this works, you will understand why you react the way you do. Both the good and the bad.
- **Abundant energy:** Is your energy being zapped by stress and you are not even aware of it? Learn the signs and the treatments.
- **Meditation and mindfulness for the soul:** Learn the basics of meditation and mindfulness for everyday use. No blank mind required.
- **What happens in vagus:** An introduction to the underestimated vagus nerve and how to harness its power.

- **Magic of intention:** How to improve your day by simply asking for a good day in the right way.

Like to know how Stress Soulutions Seminars and Workshops can benefit your people and organisation? Visit my website www.lifesoulcoaching.com.au.

Offer 2

Stress Soulutions Online Course

Feeling stressed? This instant and permanent stress reduction online course could be the solution!

Learn the skills and techniques you need to master stress anytime, any place with this self-paced online training course.

This course will help you to understand the impacts of stress and give you the tools and techniques you need to live your best life. **We'll go deep into every aspect of self-care, stress and mind and body wellness.**

The 12 modules of the course cover:

- **Healthy relaxed living:** Explores the undisputable connection between stress and illness and how you can achieve ultimate health throughout your life.

- **Thank your pain:** Learn the language that our bodies speak so you can understand and interpret the messages and act early to stay well.
- **Feel good formula:** Understanding the science behind cancer prevention. This could save your life.
- **Busting the myths:** Your genes do not determine your health. So, now you know… what next? Learn to utilise neuroscience and accelerate your strengths.
- **The art of following your intuition:** The most powerful person in your life is you. Learn simple but powerful techniques to harness this.
- **Utilising energy medicine:** Combining old and new knowledge, to determine what is best for you.
- **Change your life with NLP:** Neurolinguistic programming can be simple, fun and life-changing.
- **Your sensational nervous system:** When you learn how this works, you will understand why you react the way you do. Both the good and the bad.
- **Abundant energy:** Is your energy being zapped by stress and you are not even aware of it? Learn the signs and the treatments.
- **Meditation and mindfulness for the soul:** Learn the basics of meditation and mindfulness for everyday use. No blank mind required.
- **What happens in vagus:** An introduction to the underestimated vagus nerve and how to harness its power.

Offer 2

- **Magic of intention:** How to improve your day by simply asking for a good day in the right way.

Visit my website to find out more www.lifesoulcoaching.com.au or email life.soul@bigpond.com to start the course today!

Offer 3

Stress Soulutions 1:1 Coaching

Imagine no longer questioning your purpose or underestimating your power...

This transformational one-on-one coaching starts with a full lifestyle assessment questionnaire before we meet.

In this mind and body review we'll examine where you are now and most importantly, **where you want to be**.

Six and 12 session packages are available.

I work best with those who regularly look after others such as nurses, mothers and carers who may need a life tune-up.

During the coaching sessions we'll explore any issues you may have with anxiety, depression, confidence, weight loss and children – and help you bring more magic to your life.

Testimonials

Reading this book is something you need to do for yourself, not only to help with stress but also self-discovery. I now feel so much better prepared to deal with stress and have been able to pinpoint a couple of important dynamics that I now have the power to change. I am able to reflect and evaluate my own personal stressors, to think about how I can improve management as well as promote positive changes and build resiliency.

I particularly liked the fresh approach to the subject exploring the impact of stress on the body and looking at different strategies to control it. Niomi's style is dynamic, passionate, fun and very engaging. She communicates with genuine warmth and exudes empathy. The gifted insight and real-life experiences expressed in her writing provide the means for the reader to be their own instruments.

I enjoyed the whole experience and how it enabled me to recognise those things that I am already doing and encouraged me to

continue exploring new possibilities. I've changed the way I approach my day-to-day routine and my attitude and now recognise that a lot of my stress is brought on by my perception.

The book is definitely an eye opener and wake-up call, it gave me so much useful and practical information that I will carry with me forever. It reminded me to 'stop and smell the roses' and gave me the tools to help manage my stress and stay in the present.

The author without a doubt walks the walk. She is professional, wise, sensitive, empathetic, compassionate and both her belief and hope are inspiring. Her direct delivery of information is gentle with a very calming, soothing and validating style that is clearly full of passion. This read is spot on and will positively change your life.

Jayne Messias, Clinical Nurse

Having known Niomi for over 20 years, I am so glad she has compiled her knowledge into this wonderful book. As nurses, we deal with stress every day. As much as we love the work we do, due to the emotional and physical constraints, many of us work part-time. Anxiety and depression are unfortunately too common, in both health professionals and patients, and often much of my day is spent supporting young nurses and doctors.

Testimonials

Niomi shares her experience and insight on many non-medical treatments for pain relief and stress that have the potential to make a huge difference in the lives of so many. This book provides a timely introduction to the possibilities of prevention and alternative therapies.

Melanie Meneaud, Registered Nurse

Having suffered from depression and anxiety for many years, I am often looking for ways to reduce stress in my life. After being stuck in survival mode for so long, I am constantly trying to get over that 'hump' that stops me enjoying my life and the many blessings I have in it, to its full extent.

Too often carers and empaths take on the emotions and pain of those who surround them and are not taught how to look after their own emotional wellbeing, resulting in poor health. This book reinforces the use of mindfulness and many relaxation techniques to help with stress which I am familiar with and have found very useful but have not used consistently.

The way Niomi has explained and applied science to stress, has made me feel more connected with myself. By understanding the physiological reactions of the body in emotionally draining situations, it gives us more power to control our psychological reactions and reduce the adverse effects on our body.

My mind has been opened to try different techniques to control stress and anxiety and truly make some 'me' time. Niomi offers practical advice and methods that can easily fit into everyday life. I am looking forward to following the actions set out at the end of each chapter as a guide to better my wellbeing, make it a priority and enjoy the wonderful world I live in.

Ali Owen, Registered Nurse and Mother

www.ingramcontent.com/pod-product-compliance
Lightning Source LLC
Chambersburg PA
CBHW071733080526
44588CB00013B/2012